GOD
IS MY
SOUL
PROVIDER

Mattie Pearl Walton

GOD

IS MY

SOUL

PROVIDER

God Is Everything That You Want Him to Be and More

MINISTER MATTIE PEARL WALTON

GOD IS MY SOUL PROVIDER
GOD IS EVERYTHING THAT YOU WANT HIM TO BE AND MORE

Gotham Books

30 N Gould St.
Ste. 20820, Sheridan, WY 82801
https://gothambooksinc.com/

Phone: 1 (307) 464-7800

© 2023 *Mattie Pearl Walton*. All rights reserved.

No part of this book may be reproduced, stored in a retrieval system, or transmitted by any means without the written permission of the author.

Published by Gotham Books (September 1, 2023)

ISBN: 979-8-88775-453-6 (P)
ISBN: 979-8-88775-454-3 (E)

Because of the dynamic nature of the Internet, any web addresses or links contained in this book may have changed since publication and may no longer be valid.

The views expressed in this work are solely those of the author and do not necessarily reflect the views of the publisher, and the publisher hereby disclaims any responsibility for them.

Contents

Acknowledgements 1

My Life Growing Up And Being Chosen As
A Minister Of God.. 2

Take Time Out For Jesus And Yourself 22

Work Your Problems Out With God 60

Endnotes 128

ACKNOWLEDGEMENTS

I am writing this book because God has inspired me to do so. I want to dedicate it to the whole world. I have been encouraged by my husband, pastor, and friend, Billy Dean Walton. I want to give thanks to my church family at Mount Zion West located in Alexander City for their encouragement and support. I want to thank my children, grandchildren, sisters and my brother for their support. Everyone is always encouraging me to go ahead and preach the word. I was encouraged to preach it in season and out of season. I was encouraged to preach the word when anyone would listen and even when they fore bared against it. I pray that as you read my book, you receive a blessing spiritually. I pray that the days ahead of you be saturated with God's endless love, peace, and protection.

MY LIFE GROWING UP AND BEING CHOSEN AS A MINISTER OF GOD

This is a book about my life. God has inspired me to write a preach word, of my life. I just wanted to share a few things with you. To do this it could make things better for me and for others. My life was horrible. We lived in a house you could look up through the sealing and count the stars. We could look under the house and count the chickens. I did not have much but I was always thankful for my life. Deep down in my heart I always believed God was going to bring me out. I slept in a bed with three sisters we were stacked just like a can of sardines. I turned over when I got ready to get up. When I grew up, I went to school. I walked to school about two miles. When I got there the other children were already out on break. I wore old high heels to school. My dad took those high heel shoes and took them to the shoe shop, and had that man to take the heels off and put a low heel on them. That made the toe stands up. He wanted me to wear them with socks, I did not wear them. I went down in the woods and I cried all day long, but I was too young to quit school. So I kept on trying. I stayed out for awhile, and then went back. If I had not gone back to school, they would have put my parents in jail. When I was older I went to pick cotton to buy shoes to wear to school. By this time, I was so far behind, but I went back but still could not go when it was time to go to work in the field. I had to stay at home to work I went when it rained. I chopped cotton and when we finished ours, we then had to help the neighbors with their cotton. My dad once told my sister and me that we could have a field of cotton by ourselves. We were so happy.

I picked my field first, and then I helped my sister pick her field. My dad took all of the money; we did not get a penny from the cotton. He took both of our money. That is when I knew that I had to do voluntary work. Not looking for pay, not at home, I had this friend at school; she would let me use her books to do my homework if I would do hers too. I could not keep her books long, so I put them under my head to sleep at night, because someone told me if you sleep with them under your head you would not forget what you read. Things had got so bad. I would go in the woods If would pray and ask God, Why are these things happening to me? I did not understand, now I know, I was supposed to preach at the age of twelve years old. I gave up the best of my life. I did not want to obey God. You can do this too, but do not try this. When I got older I went in to a stage of shame. I was ashamed of everybody and everything. I stayed like that for about twenty-five years. I did not understand why I was cut-off from the pleasure of life, because of not obeying God. I did not want anyone to come near me. I stayed hid. I would not go out to play with anyone in school or out of school. I was living in a world of darkness, and gloominess. I felt like I was in a bottle with the top on it. Everyday my teacher would ask me if I was alright, I would say yes. She would ask if I wanted some of her lunch, I would say no because I thought someone else would see me talking to her. I wanted what she had; I was ashamed to take it. By this time my dad moved us about five miles from the school. We still had to walk to school. Our mom walked with us there and back. When we got there, sometimes they were already turned out of school for the day, so the next day we stayed at home to rest. My mom was afraid to let us go alone, and she was afraid to stay at home by herself because we lived at the end of the road. We got back home about dust dark. None of us attended school regularly. It was not important to our parents, especially my dad. He had already made my brothers some shoes out of enter tubs out of a car. They were tied with some wire and he made him wear them. By this time my mom was very angry with my dad. She was in town one night and my dad came by, but he did not look at my mom. She picked up a rock and threw it at him. She struck the heel of his shoe and knocked the whole heel off his shoe. He turned around that night, he came back and gave my mom money and went home. Every time my dad did not come home and do right, my brother would say to my mom get a rock. My dad did not believe in going to school or going to church. If my mom and I went to church, we had to break in when we got back if he did not let us in the house, and then the fight was on for the rest of the night. It got so bad once, we had to sleep in our clothes to be ready to stop them from fighting. This went on every Friday and Saturday night. Once my dad and mom had a fight, my dad left home that night, my mom and I had went out into the woods to get wood to cook on a wood stove and when we made a fire my dad came in the house and poured water on the fire and put it out. By the this time my dad had moved up to a place where we were so far out we had to leave home at five o'clock to catch the bus so we would not go out to the bus stop so you could not see us. We would sit back trying to hide from the other people. Sometimes just before the bus came we were all asleep. We would hear the bus when it pulled off we would then get up and go back home. They would then put us back to work. If I learned anything, I learned how to work. Whatever season we were in farming that is what we ate. We raised everything in the garden and fields. Corn season we ate corn, peas, that is what we ate. Potatoes we ate. Potatoes, syrup we ate syrup. We never changed up. We used the Lord off our hogs to fix our hair, brown paper sacks to roll our hair. Every Friday they had dances at the school. I never had a dime to go to any of the dances, but I did not want to go in because I did not want the other children to smell what I had on my head. My family was the talk of the town already. People laughed at us, but we kept on going, we did not have money. When the candy man would come, we had told him so long we did not have any money, he would still stop, he would say, I just want to hear you say it. My mom would say, say what, just say I do not have any money. So finally the candy man would just ride by and throw us some candy out of the window of the car. We would say Thank God for the blessing. My mom acted just like we had enough money to buy cleaning for the house. Everything was okay. We walked to the store just to buy washing powder, soap, Clorox, with not enough money to get a cold drink. I would see my mom go in the woods and sit down on a stump; I would find her down there. I asked her what is wrong. She would say I am hurting. I ask her, where are you hurting? She would say my heart is hurting. I would then ask again who made your heart hurt? She said you do not understand one day you will. I would always hear her say the Lord will make a way. We washed from sun up to sun down. When we finished, we had one outfit to wear, so when my brothers grew up they started to work when they got paid they gave my dad money every week. He still did not bring any money home. He spent his and their money. When they found out what was going on, they stopped giving him money. Then we had to stay dressed to stop dad and my brothers from fighting every Friday and Saturday night. My brothers would say where the groceries are, he would say there it is. He would have about ten to twelve cases of beer and from that the fight was on. There were times my sister and I would eat raw peas and rice. We would go in the woods looking for pecans and whatever we could find.

We went fishing trying to make a living at Christmas time. We knew what we would get: one apple, one orange, and a few nuts in a bag no cake, one piece of peppermint candy. One year we did not get that, but no one ever knew it. Out of it all we went through, I still did not hear anyone pray, so one day I told my sisters, come on and lets go to the woods and pray. Nothing happen, so I got brave one day, I said tonight lets sing a song, if you all sing, I will preach, so they did. They sang and I preached. I was preaching thy shall not kill, at the time. That's all I knew, but I knew, it was time to do some thing, so after that my dad told me to get up one morning and kill a chicken, I got up but I did not kill that chicken I held that chicken until day light, my dad came out there and ask me what was wrong that I had not kill the chicken I told my dad the bible said thy shall not kill he then went in the house and told my mom, what I had said. He was getting ready to get onto me. My mom said let her alone she is very strange. My dad walk away that night my dad look at me he said what do you mean that is a chicken I said to him I know that He said as much chicken as you can eat. I told him that chicken I ate was already dead by this time I am very tired. I was tired of holding a lamp to do my homework, I held a light for my sisters, and she held it for me. I was getting to be a teenager. I went and got a job babysitting. I stop going to school. I was working making three dollars a day. I gave my mom half of what I made every week. I can remember when we owned our first refrigerator and our first couch. We were borrowing ice from the neighbors, and I had to run to get there before it melted; I told my mom I am tired now. Everyday my mom wanted to quilt a quilt in one day, and we did. So one night my mom and dad got into a fight before he started at my mom he put me out of the door. When they started I was walking down the road. I heard the noise, I then turned around. I ran back they were fighting. I ran into the door and kicked the door down. My dad pushes me back out the door. My mom told me to go on. I left home. I went to stay with my brother, and sister-in-law. It was not much better there. My brother said you are welcome to stay with us. My brother said to me he said I will buy for you and my kids too. It will not be any different with you. He said I will not buy for them unless I buy for you too. If I do not have enough to buy for all of you, I will not buy anything for anyone. I stayed with them for four years. He did not buy anyone anything. When he got paid, he did not come home, so he told his wife I do not know why I can not come home when I get paid. So he said, this Friday when I get paid I am going to tell my boss man to bring me home before I cash my check. You will get this check. My sister-in-law was so happy all that week. So my brother he did come home. The boss man brought him home. WE looked out the door my brother was running back up the road behind his boss man's truck. We did not see him for days He came back and told us he said I couldn't help it doing this. This time my brother didn't allow my sister-in-law to go anywhere. She stayed at home around the clock. She would send us through the woods to get food from the neighbors. She would save him food when she cooked. My sister-in-law would sit around with her head tied up and wouldn't go anywhere. We didn't get to go to church or to town. She would send us to get sweet potatoes out of people fields, turnip greens or whatever we could find. We were lucky we didn't get caught.

One day my sister-in-law got tired and decided that she wasn't going to do this any longer. We had borrowed until it was sickness. She started fixing herself up one night my brother came home and she was dressed up and he jumped on her. She took a piece of wood and knocked him out. When he came to himself he told her from now on we will go out together and they did. We were at home alone every Friday night. It had gotten to where we didn't know what to do again. I told them I said lets us pray and sing, so we did. I told them I will preach. So while I was preaching, my brother and his wife came up to the window. They didn't come in right then; they stayed outside and listened to us singing and praising God. So after awhile they came in, my sister-in-law started to cry she said, I will never drink another drop as long as I live. So far she hasn't so later on she started going to church. She told us that she was ashamed when she heard us inside preaching and praying. She received the Holy Ghost and she is still preaching the word. Only if one take a step. That's all it takes. I still go to see them. Like they are my parents, my sister-in-law, then started picking cotton for an older man along with other people he hired us. This man would put his cotton in my stack and pay for it too. So after awhile this man started to come back at night to see me. My brother told him he said you are too old for my sister; she is just sixteen years old. He told my brother I don't care if she is not but eight hours old I will be back to see her. When my brother couldn't stop him from coming to see me, he went and told my mom and she came to get me. I hid in the woods until they left. I went back to my brother's house. I did this so many times. I told the man please doesn't come, but he kept on coming. I would hide when he came over. I would tell them to go to the door and tell him I wasn't at home. They would do that, and he would say okay, thank louver much. He would turn around and leave. Then I would get dressed and go up the road. When I had gone about a whole mile, he would rise up out of the ditch, and say there go my baby. He then would follow my everywhere I went. Once a young man came to see me and he told him, if you don't leave here, I will blow your head off even with your shoulders. The young man left and didn't come back. He told this man, if you ever come back, I will throw a match stem at your head so hard and if it don't hit you, the air from the match will kill you, that's how powerful I am he would say. Please believe me. This old man started bringing me food to my house. I was eating it, I felt like this was the end of my life. I found out I couldn't get rid of him. I started talking to him. I would think he was gone he would be in the window. One night I looked out of the window and my eyes caught his eyes. I almost fainted. He came back in the house and he said that's the way I will catch you if you mess up. I knew this man had already killed a man. I was young and afraid of him anyway. He would say I killed one, I will kill two, don't let the next one be you. I would sit up at night wondering how to get out, no one would help me. He told me, you will be my wife after all this I ended up marrying him. Talk about trouble, all hell broke loose. After running from him so long, I just stopped and married him. He didn't have a car and couldn't drive either. We caught a ride to go and get married. After that, I felt like I had been in a dark room and time I came home with him, the sun came out and shine on me. I was so ashamed. I cried two weeks before I could stop crying. I knew I had messed up. I thought I was in big trouble before, but not really until I got with him. By the time we had been married one year I had one child, a girl. The next year, I had one more, a boy. I had another boy the following year after that. I had a boy and girl the year after that. I had two babies in pampers and on bottles. The next year I had another baby boy. The next year I had another girl. The next year I had another girl. The next year I had another boy. Two years later I had another boy. Six more years I had the last one a boy, at an early age. In my first marriage, my husband had to go for an operation on his eyes. He came home every two weeks with fifteen dollars. He would set up at night and watch me sleep. After he found out that he couldn't keep me hid always he then let me go get my hair fixed, but he went with me. He walked with me through the woods and he walked back with me. When he did work he brought me nice clothes, but didn't want anyone to see them but him. We stayed with his parents, when someone came over to see his parents he would close the door where we slept so no one could see me. I was in the room bur I couldn't come out. The people would ask him where is your wife we heard you were married. He would tell them she is very ashamed. When they left he would open the door he and I would go through a little trail to a small store to buy our little food. We would walk back with it and we were the talk of the town. If I looked out of the window he would ask me what are you looking for, I would say nothing, and he would say get back in here.

He was jealous too. Sometimes when he was working, but he couldn't go to work. He then let me go to work with all the children. He knew someone had to work. Someone asked me one day, why did you have so many children? I told them if it takes a whole month to load a gun there is no way it can miss a shot when it shoots. I was very sad in my heart. I went to work it took everything I made to feed my children but I didn't mind it. I was so glad to be out of the house. When it was time to go home I would go in the bathroom and shed tears before I left the job. He didn't want me to go to work, but he knew we were going to starve to death. He would sleep all day long and when I would get home he would argue all night sometimes. I would sit up all night and listen to him. I would get back up the next morning and go back to work. This went on so long until one morning I went back to work and my friend ask me did you look in the mirror before you came to work. I said yes, why? She said, do you know you have changed color? I went into the bathroom at work. I look closer to my face, and it was blue. I then look at my feet and they were too. My hands were blue as well. She went and told our boss man that I was a little sick and he called me to the office. He told me to take off and go to the doctor. Nothing that the doctor told me helped. I went home and returned back to work the next day after taking the medicine he prescribed. I was working when something hit me in the top of my head and blinds me. I went to the bathroom and waited awhile until I could go back to work. Later on I went to the doctor and he told me you been coming here along time and today I am going to tell you what the problem is. He said, you need a young man in your life. I knew that but I didn't want to try that. I was afraid to keep on going. Things got so bad and I collected demons that I thought I couldn't shake off. This is the one that almost destroyed my life. I went to the river to try to drown, but before I got there something came over me just like a rainbow. I stopped and looked around and it left me. I was in a dark place and then I turned around. I had to live with that without any help. I begin to have a mean streak in me. Everyday I felt like I wanted to fight. One day my mom was sick and my husband wouldn't let me go to see her, I got very mad. He had backed me back there in that room, I jumped up and kicked the door down and walked out. When I got back they were putting up another door. By that time I had a don't care mind. Once I got into it with someone and I got a pistol. I tried to shoot the gun and it wouldn't fire. When I laid the gun down it went off right by my leg. I sit there for about 5 hours before I could move. I sit there just saying Jesus, Jesus, thank you Jesus you didn't let it happen. I went from sad to angry from angry to mad. They sent me to a counselor. This man told me it's not anything wrong with you, but you are just an unhappy woman and it's up to you what you are going to do about. So my husband got sick, he had a stroke, and had to go to a nursing home to get cared for because he couldn't swallow anything. I went to see him almost every afternoon after I got off from work. Before He got sick, I went to get my divorce.

I got there and turned around. I didn't get it. I came back home and did the same thing all over again. I wanted to leave and get with someone else but it didn't work for me. I couldn't think about leaving him after he got sick. It was over for me leaving him then. So I settled down and that was it. I couldn't get away while he was weak. I wasn't going to leave him then either. So after all of this, the welfare, DHR, came to my house and told me that they had to take away my four youngest children. They told me that someone had reported that I was staying out at night. I did not stay away from my children, not even for one night. Not only was I taking care of my children, but I was feeding everybody's children that were around. They took them away in court that almost killed me. With in two weeks they came and told me that they found out that the people was lying to them on me. For two weeks this lady would be at my house everyday when I got home from work. One day I ask her what is going on. She said its not anything going on I was just in the neighborhood so I just stopped to check on the children, everything is okay. So in about a week later they call me in court. That day they kept them down there. They then tried to get me to come back there and get them. They said we have made a mistake in this case. I then told them that I would take them back if we would go back to court with them. They wouldn't go back in the courtroom with the case. It ended up I didn't get them back they told me said the reason we took them you had too much on you. I never let any of my children stay all night with any9ne. Not one time, I will say you can out live a lie. When all this happen, I moved away from this town. I couldn't find a job and when I did find one I had to leave home walking about five o'clock to have biscuits ready before six o'clock. I was cooking at a restaurant. I was making forty nine dollars a week at the time. I was paying two hundred dollars a month for food stamps and when this job shutdown, I then got a job making a $100 dollars a week. I then picked-up a little bit, but then I got sick. I stayed at home two years. One day my son came to the house and asked me are you going to sit here and die? He said you are taking all this medicine and it's not going through your bloodstream and its not doing you any good what so ever. I begin to think on that. One day I said I am going to try to walk to town. I got up and got dressed and when I went out the door began to get nervous. I had to sit back down. I got up again. I said, I am going to give it another try. I did, I got down the road. I got so nervous I had to sit down in the streets, but I hurried up and stood back up because I didn't want anyone to see me sitting on the streets. After I got almost well, I went back to work. I did very well for awhile. This lady passed away. I then went to work for another lady making seventy-five dollars a week. Later, I worked there about four years until this lady passed away also. By this time I was ready to try marriage again. I meet this man and we started to talk. This man was in church. So while I was talking to him, I got another job at the nursing home and I worked there two years sitting with an older lady. She was seventy-eight years old, but she could out walk me. I knew then something was wrong with me. I started praying to God. I said, Lord, something is wrong with me. Then I found out I was letting the devil destroy my life. This lady gave me courage to get married again. I said then I am not dead. I am just now ready to enjoy my life. So I went to church every Sunday. So one night my husband and I went to a church to visit. It was an old lady there. After service she came up to me and said, God said for you to preach here on the 3rd Sunday.

I said, who are you talking to? She said, I am talking to you. I said to her, Well, I haven't told anyone that I was a preacher. I said do you know who I am? She said, I don't have to know you, I am speaking what God told me to tell you and I will be looking for you. I came home wondering should I try this. I had been sick, hurting everyday, and I knew this was the only thing that would make me be free. I went on and I spoke that Sunday and when I walked out the door that day, I said, I think God for healing. I got healed after that and I caught a good hold. My load got lighter. I always did try to keep my gift hid. Someone always knew they could see Jesus in my and I would get upset about that because I didn't want to preach. My pastor had told me it's no need for you to keep running someday you will still have to do it. You can just stop crying. All you got to do is just say yes to God and everything will be already. What you doing aren't going to work he told me. He said I tried the same thing and it didn't work for me and it want work for you either. You might as well give up. My husband would say you can run but you can't hide. I thought that I had to have someone with me. Sometimes you have to go by yourself and just does what the Lord say. My husband took my out to dinner; I was so ashamed I couldn't even eat my food. I was thirty-two years old. This was my first time going out to eat. It looked like everyone in the place was looking right at me. Let me tell you, the devil will kill you and have you walking around alive and dead. My spouse was good to me if I did everything he told me to do. He left me at home and he meant for me to stay at home until he came back. If I didn't stay and he passed me on the road, he wouldn't pick me up. I would ask him, why didn't you pick me up? He would say you weren't going my way. If he passed me I would walk on home. I would ask him did you see me, He would say I wasn't looking for you. You supposed stayed at home until I came back. On Sunday, we were at church. Life wasn't good but it was so much better. I was on my way to recovering. I stopped taking everything to heart. Instead, I took it to God. Anything that doesn't settle in you can't and will not hurt you. I would go and pray the hurt would leave. I kept on going to church. If you stay with Jesus, he will stay with you. My life began to get real good. My husband got sick. We both had to stay at home from the church. That's when I found out that you don't have to stay in church everyday, just give God your life and stand on the word wherever you are. Just live one day at a time. Don't make Satan any promises. He will try and make you follow through with them. Satan will tell you if you don't follow through that you are scared. You should rather be scared than dead. I went through things but God kept me. It didn't matter how angry I got I never forgot to pray. Prayer still stands good to everyone. Once I tried to stab a man but God stuck my arm with something like lightening and my arm went down. My hand flew wide open and I sit there all night trying to figure out what that was. I was so afraid. I couldn't go to bed. I got up the next morning and I dropped everything I picked up. I was so embarrassed. I didn't know what to do. Its not the only one that go up the highest, its the one go down the lowest and no man ever been down too low that God can't pick him up and no man been so far up that God can't bring him down. You can go as far down as you can and rise above the situation. If you want to see a change in your life, you have to make it happen. You can't change anything but you, and you have to let God do that for you. I found out I couldn't change anything.

When my husband got bedridden and I had to take care of him, the doctors told me I need to put him in a nursing home. I walked in his office that day and told them, when I get where I can't walk, then you send him to a nursing home, but until that happens, he will be at home with me. I kept my vows. It wore me down, but God raised my back up. It got to a point that I didn't even get undressed. I sit up night after night. I did this so long that it started getting easy for me. When God is in something it will work, because he will give you strength. I am a witness. Not only did God keep my body healed, but he also kept my mind healed too. Once I stayed at home two years and I didn't have enough strength to comb my hair. My daughters would have to comb my hair for me. I couldn't keep my arms up to do it. When I took a shower, I would be out of breath before I could get to my chair. I overcame that and went back to work. I never been to a liquor store but I was still on my way to hell. I never went to bed drunk, but I was walking around drunk until I made the change in my life. I was tired of hurting. Once I got sick and went to the hospital and had an operation. The doctor told me that I had a 55% chance of living. I told that doctor, I am not going to die because I got a job I have to do and I can't send no one else to do it for me. Then my husband passed away. I was so lost. This is when I found out that I had to go a little deeper in the word of God. I had Jesus close to me, but after he passed, I had to get him on the e inside to keep going. Sometimes we can have other things before God he told us in the word. We shouldn't have anything before him. When you promise God something, if no one else tries to help you, you still have to do it on your own. We will be judged one by one. We are supposed to love Jesus first. When Jesus was calling me, I did everything in the world to keep from hearing his voice. I went down to the railroad track and stood there. The train came. I could still hear God speaking. This begins to trouble my mind. Sometimes we can have a sickness and no man can find it. This is when you can find out that you are and what you want. You will then start seeking the Lord for yourself. It will come a time that man can't help you. Things get out of the hand of man, just like they are now. Jesus will straighten it out; it is going to take him to do it. When we are in trouble it's always not our fault. I don't find a fault in God. Once, I was out in the world. I begin to pray, I was lying in my bed one night and I was asking God to help me and I saw some huge hands appear in my room. It came in my window and it came all the way to me. I reached up to catch it, and I heard a voice that was saying not yet. The hand went back out the window. I got up and ran out the door. The hand went back in the sky and darkened everything. It was so dark that I couldn't find my way back in my house. I began praying, I was calling Jesus. After awhile, it came back to a normal dark. Then I went back in my house. Visit there all night I was so afraid. I always knew God had a calling on my life. I didn't want that. Once, I was home alone, this sister called me and asked me what are you doing?

I replied I am not doing anything. She said that's your problem then she told me to go get the Bible and just walk through the house. I asked her what I need to turn to. She said just walk in every room in your house, God want to speak to you. So I did that, but before I got into the last room the spirit of the Lord spoke to me and said, this is what God want you to do just do it, carry his word. The spirit of God got on me. I ran out the back door. I fell down on my knees and started to repent. I came up shouting the victory, and I praised God all the way back. She told me just preach, this is all you have to do, and things will change for you. She said aren't you tired of suffering? From that day I could see a change in my life. I went on then. My husband passed away. I was lost for about eight months. I could lay down at night and dose off to sleep. My nerves were so bad during this time of his suffering. My feet would jump out from under me. I would just get up and stay up all night. People would ask me how you can do this. I answered and said, God is doing it for me. At your strongest, you are never able to take care of yourself, it takes God. Without him, we are not able to make one step. When my husband passed away, I had to go back to work to pay his burial without anyone's help. It took me a whole year to pay this bill. You can do all things through Christ. Nothing, without him, whatever work you do, you will get paid for it good or bad. What is done in the dark, will come to light. You get a double pay. I heard to us pray and wait on the results and don't worry. If you pray, you don't have to worry, why pray and then worry.

TAKE TIME OUT FOR JESUS AND YOURSELF

Take time out in life for Jesus and yourself. This is for you. Take time for Jesus. Let him do the speaking and you do the listening. After all, he knows what is best for you, so in all ways acknowledge him. He will direct thy path. Take time with your spouse and you can make it or you can break it. You have to make a choice. Love started with love. Charity starts at home. If things are going wrong, sit down and talk about it and straighten it out. You cannot solve a problem that you are not aware of. Jesus took time to come all the way down through forty-two generations for you and me. Jesus work by time and on time. He took time to go down in hell to give those people souls a chance to be saved. He took the time to come all the way back to earth to give us a chance. He took time to teach men. He yet takes time with us. He took time to go back to his father. He took time to send back the Holy Ghost so we would have a leader and a teacher to give us guides us into all truth. This is why it is so very important to have the Holy Ghost. Most people think that is not so, this something is just being said, this is real. Jesus took time to go to the grave and he raised Lazarus from the grave although he was dead. (St. John 11-43). God will raise you from your spiritual death and put life back into you. Jesus took time to send Ezekiel down to the valley to put breath into the dry bones (Ezekiel 37-4). So if you will hear the word and let it shake you, and let it wake you, it will make you don not let your wood God fool you. Wake up because this is true. If you couldn't see, you would still know the day the Lord is at hand. I am not trying to scare you. It is time to wake up and hear what the spirit is saying to the church. If you can read, you don't have any excuse. Jesus took them to the cross and didn't read neither did he say see. He said here the word of God. So if you are blind, just hear the word. It is better not to hear the word, then to hear it and not do it. If you hear and didn't do, you are taking demotion to your own soul.

When Ezekiel went down to the valley of the dry bones, he told them to hear the word of the Lord. Do not be a loser, receive the word. Jesus took time to go to the woman at the well. He let her know that she wasn't to far down that he couldn't pick her up and put her on the right road, although she had five husbands. If she would just have one, it would have been the same. This woman spoke out and said, I have five husbands and neither one is mine. It is time to tell the truth. Hell is hot and it isn't getting cooler, but getting larger (Matthew 5-22). This verse talks about being cast in to Hell's fire (Luke 16:24) Tormented in the flame, and if nothing is not in flame, it is not anything burning and if there is not a flame, it is not a fire. Unlock your mind. Jesus is still giving us time to get it right with him. When the scribes and Pharisees brought unto Jesus a woman, taken in adultery: they sat her in the mist and they said unto the master, this woman was taken in adultery in the very act. Moses recommended that such should be stoned, but what safest thy; this they said tempting him that they might have to accuse him. Jesus stooped down and with his finger wrote on the ground as though he heard them not. When they kept asking, he lifted himself up and said unto them, he that is without sin cast the first stone. He stooped down again and wrote on the ground, but he never spelled the words he wrote, because he was waiting on his father to speak. Sometimes this is our problem; we don't wait on Jesus to speak to us. Sometimes you can wait too late, this is why it is so important to wait on the Lord. Rest in the Lord, he will direct you. One thing, people don't know is Jesus doesn't beat you up, he picks you up and keeps you up, if you wan to be kept up. But Jesus love and hate, he loves you, but he hates sin. No own would do what Jesus did if they could. Jesus didn't have to die on the cross, but he did. He died for our sin. It wasn't the nails that kept him on the cross, it was the love he had for us that kept him there (John 15:13). No greater love than a man that would lay down his life for his friends, ye are my friends, if ye do whatsoever I command you. If you don't do what he commands you, you are a enemy to me. If you are a friend of the world, you are not my friend, because you do not do what I say. The world loves its own. (Joshua 24:15) said. If it seems evil unto you to serve the Lord, choose this day that ye will serve. Whether it is the God on which your Father served or that were o the other side of the flood or the Gods of the Amorites in whose land ye shall dwell. But as for me and my house, we will serve the Lord. This is the question: Who do you love? Who will you choose for your God? Don't let it be said too late. It is about time for the closing of the gate, make up your mind. It is a family memory of mind now. Don't let this chance slip through. Don't let this happen to you. Why not trust the one you can rest assures loves you. He gave his life for you, he didn't ask us to give up anything but our sinful life, which is not hard to do. The ways of transgression is hard. That is when you don't want to do it. Jesus willingly gave up his life for us. They didn't take his life, he gave it up. Now, who will you choose? Joshua couldn't speak for his household. He said, this is for me, me, and me. You have to do this for yourself. Mother can't help you on this, daddy can't help you, brother can't help you, sister would love to, but can't. They can only give you the word of God.

Take heed when you hear, hear this, when it come your way, it might not come another day because Jesus said the day you here my voice harden and not your heart. He didn't say the days you hear my voice. That means you could hear only one time. Don't do like Jonas, he made the wrong choice and went the wrong way. He didn't stay long; he came back by the mighty hand of God. You don't have to be made to obey, does it willingly? Some people today are paying for a trip to the wrong place: when Jesus is trying to give you a free trip to the right way. Some people are going the wrong way because someone is paying you to go. You will perish with your money, on the Dimmed road. It might not be but a few people on this narrow way, but I want to be one of them. I know in the last days. Perils time will come when men will not endure sound doctrine, but I believe someone will hear the word of God. They might not hear a word, but someone will hear the word of God. His word has power in it. Someone might offer a word. That want work. God's word changed me. If he could do it for me, he can change anybody. I was heart hard-headed with a stiff neck. Didn't know anything about love, but I was always looking for love, passing it everyday. I was looking in man and I didn't know it wasn't there. Man will let you down. Jesus picked me up just when I was almost ready to give up. Don't ever give up on God. If you be put in the fire, stay there you want get burned. Jesus is there with you. What he did for others he will do for you (Jeremiah 4:1). To the backsliding children, God said, I will heal your backsliding if thy will return unto me, and if thy will put away thine abominations out of my sight. Then shalt thou not be removed. God is saying you can stand. Stick and stay if you walk in his way. It is not your way, it is God's way, because he said, I am the way, the truth, and the life. That leaves us out, get in the way (John 14:6). Jesus said, you have heard how I heal the sick, you have heard how I gave sight to the blind, you heard how I raised the dead from the grave, and you still looking for a way? It is only one way, get in it, it won't be another way. Believe the word of God. Jesus is Christ. No one else (Acts 18:24). Apollo's taught the word knowing only the baptism of John. If you teach that you know, that is a start from God. Just like a car, you can pour gas all day, but without the motor, the car won't start. First, you become sorry, then you repent. Next you believe that you received. Next, you got to receive. Then it will come to pass. This is why Apollo's was at Corinth. Paul having passed through the upper coast came to Ephesus, and finding certain disciples, and he said unto them: Have ye received the Holy Ghost since ye believed? And they said unto him, we have not so much as heard whether there will be any Holy Ghost. He said unto them, unto what then was ye baptized? And they said unto John baptism, then said Paul, John verily baptized with the baptism of Repentance, saying unto the people, that they should believe on him who should come a filter him. That is on Christ Jesus. When they heard this, they were baptized in the name of the Lord Jesus and when Paul had laid his hands upon them the Holy Ghost came on them and they spoke with tongues and prophesized. After this, you can speak the word of God. Maybe someone have told you the Holy Spirit is enough, but this is not so. The spirit will get in you and you can feel it, but the Holy Ghost will get in you and live in you. You can feel a lot of things. When you go down town shopping, but if you don't have what it takes to pay for it, you have to leave it there. When you go to church and hear the word of God it will make you fill real good. When you leave the church, it is gone.

So bring it home with you. The way to bring it home, it must be in foul: daily the Holy Ghost and with faith. It is time to get faith like Moses. Stretch out your rod and you might not have a rod in our hand. You should have a rod in your heart. A rod of faith, stretch it out. Use what you got, if you don't use what you have, Jesus will take it back. You will hear people say, I am going to get back what the devil took from me. Sometimes Jesus takes it back. If the devil took something from you, you shouldn't mind. You don't need what the devil have. To do a work for Jesus. God gave you everything that you will need, and what you need is the word of God. The word saves, the word heals all matters of sickness. Jesus will give you everything you need. What will you give him? Will you give him your body? (Romans 12:1) Paul said, I be seeking you therefore; brethren by the mercies of God that ye present your bodies a living sacrifice holy acceptable unto God which is your reasonable service. This is all for you, you have not did God no favors, your body belong to God anyway. Jesus said; present your body a living sacrifice, not when you are dead neither when you are on your sick bed. Someone asked me one day, Can God save you on your death bed? I told him, God can do whatever he wants to because he is God, but that is to close a call for me. He told us in his word, our ways are not his ways, neither our thought can never know the mind of God. He said as high is heaven above the earth, that is how much higher his ways are than ours. (Acts 6:3) Wherefore brethren, look out among out and find seven men of honest report full of the Holy Ghost and wisdom that we may appoint over this business. I am the business for Jesus, but we will give ourselves continually prayer and to the ministry of the word. I will tell you everything God give me (Jeremiah 1:5). Before I formed thee in the belly I knew thee and before thou calmest forth out of the womb I sanctified thee, and I ordained thee, a prophet unto the nations then said I, ah Lord God. Behold, I can not speak for I am a child, but the Lord said unto me, say not I am a child, for thou shalt go to all that I shall send thee and whatsoever I command thee, thou shall speak. I was just like Jeremiah, I wanted to do everything but preach. I said, Lord I cannot speak very well, I wanted God to choose my sister's because they could speak better than I could, so God called to move my sisters' to preach. I was happy, but God kept on speaking to me, Preach, I was saying, two should be enough out of one family. That didn't help me though. I kept on going. I knew I was running from the Lord. So every Tuesday, I would call all the children in the neighborhood and I would teach them the Bible. I would feed them. I got a little more worried everyday. Jesus feed five thousand, but they still had to receive Jesus, and someone had to teach the word of God and someone had to do it now. More so now more than ever, because of the sin that is in the world now. When God told Jeremiah to go, be not afraid of there faces, for I am with thee, to deliver thee, smith the Lord, then the Lord put forth his hand and touched my mouth and the Lord said, unto me, Behold I have put my words in thy mouth, see I have this day set thee over the nations, and over the kingdoms to root out and to pull down, and to destroy and to throw down, to build and to plant the mess that is going on in the world. God want his people to get busy in the word of God, root out everything that is not like God, and pull it down. How can you pull it down, don't support it, let it come down, destroy it, let the Holy Ghost burn it.

The Holy Ghost is fire and it came to burn up everything that is not of God. When you burn it, throw it down, and then you can say it is finished. I don't want it again. This is the way you put it under your feet. As long as you feed it, it will grow, dig it up by the root.

Don't wait on Satan to loose you, loose him, you can walk around with malice, strife, and hate in you r heart. Give it up, give an honest report, and free yourself. The truth will come out anyway. Everything that is done in the dark will come to the light. God is not mocked whatsoever. What a man sows, that he shall reap. (Galatians 6:7). Whatever is in your heart is already known to God and soon it will be known of man. You can do good deeds, but if it is not from your heart, it will not profit anything for you (Ephesians 6:11). Put on the whole armor of God that ye maybe able to stand against thaw wise of the devil. We wrestle not against flesh and blood, but against principalities against powers against the rulers of the darkness of this world against spiritual sickness in high places. Therefore, take unto you the whole armor of God that ye maybe able to withstand in the evil day and having done all to stand. Stand therefore, having your Lions girl about with truth and having on the breath plate of righteousness and your feet shod with the preparation of the gospel of peace above all, taking the shield of faith, where with the ye shall be able to quench all the fiery darts of the wicked and take the helmet of salvation and the sword of the spirit which is the word of God. Praying always with all prayer and supplication in the spirit and watching there unto wit all supplication for all saints and for me that utterance may be given me that I may open my mouth boldly to make known the mystery of the gospel. Whatever we learn, it is not all written in the book. Something's are revelations by the spirit of God. It is given by faith, use what faith you have and you will see faith moves God

(Matthew 17:20). Said if you have faith of a grain of mustard seed, you can speak to the mountain and say, Remove; hence, to yonder a place, and it shall remove and nothing shall be impossible unto you. You don't know what faith will do until you stretch out on it. When the fisherman was fishing, they had fished all night long, Jesus sit down and taught them. When Jesus left speaking he said unto Simon, Launch out into the deep and let down your nets for a draught and Simon answering said, unto him, Master we have toiled all night and have taken nothing; never the less at thy word, I will let down the net. The fisherman didn't catch anything until they obeyed God's word (Luke 5:1). This is why things are so hard with us, we are working too hard because we try to do on our own, if we wait on Jesus to speak it will work. We are working, but to close to the bank. Jesus is saying today stretch out, reach out on faith, go a little further. Go down a little deeper for a draught. Not only will you catch fish, you will catch the souls of men, if we fish with the right bait and the bait is our life. Don't let your good be evil spoken of, hold a light so someone can come out by your light. Go out looking for something. God said his word want go out void it will accomplish what it is sent out to do. If you have faith, believe in God. Without faith, it is impossible to please God. By faith Abraham was saved when he gave himself up to God just by obeying. (22:4). Then on the 3rd day Abraham lifted up his eyes and saw the place afar off and he said unto his young men, Abide ye here with the ass and I and the lad will go yonder and worship and come again to you.

While Abraham and his son were on there way to this place, Issuance asked his father and he said, my father and he said here and I my son and he said, Behold, the fire and the wood but where are the lamb, for a burnt offering, and Abraham said my son. God will provide him a lamb for a burnt offering. So they went together. Then he said, we will return unto them again. He knew God Sometimes you can't speak things, you just have to act upon them. It will be times that you can stand back and see the power of God go forth. Faith is not something you can see (Hebrew 11:1) Said, now faith is the substance of things hoped for, the evidence of things not yet seen. By faith, the elders obtained a good report. Through faith we understand that the world was framed by the word of God so that things which are seen were not made of things which do not appear. So if we see what we want, we don't have to hope for it, we already have it. You speak it to come and have faith it will happen. If we speak with doubt, it will not happen. By faith, Jericho walls fell down, but it didn't fall on the first round and your wall will not fall on the first round but keep on going. One day it will come down, and if trouble is in your way, keep marching and don't five up. Don't get tired along the way just when you want to give up, it could be one more day. You might feel like you are the only one marching, but keep on. You will be the one to finish the march. Peter walked on the water as long as he kept his eyes on Jesus, but when he took his eyes off of him, he went down. He lost his faith in Jesus. This is what happens to us today, we have taken our eyes of f of Jesus. Lets put our eyes back on our help. Jesus is the only one that can help and without him we will fall. We can't fall too far down that Jesus will not pick us up. He want do it against your will. He is still saying who so ever will let them come. He that cometh to me I will in no wise cast them out. You don't have to pay your way to Jesus, you can come broke. Just come with your whole heart and mind. Man love you because of, Jesus love you in spite of, but hate that sin in you. Make up your mind today while you still have a chance. It is not so bad to go down as long as you know you are down there. Acknowledge your wrong, and then you can come back. Jesus will forgive you and receive you back (Psalms 37:23). The steps of a good man are ordered by the Lord and he is delighted in his way. Though he falls, he shall not be utterly cast down for the Lord upheld him with his hand. Now, if you be ordered by man, you will make some crocket steps on the way. So let Jesus lead you all the way. When Moses leads the children of Israel out of Egypt that was by faith his steps were ordered by God. See man can have a look alike but it is false. When Moses stretch his rod and it became a serpent, Pharaoh his rod and it became a serpent also, but what you need to look at Moses serpent ate up Pharaoh Serpent because it was power in Moses serpent. There is no power in no other name but in Jesus Christ. In that name every knee is going to bow, every tongue shall confess that Jesus is Lord. No other name given under the Heaven whereby men must be saved. I might not be able to be your president. I don't have enough man's wisdom, but God gave me enough of his wisdom to tell you and the president, set your house in order because time is wining up. I would not tell this if I didn't have to. I want to be delivered too. I can't be the vice president but I can give you some advice on the word of God. I can't be your governor; I don't understand what to do.

I may not be able to be your mayor, but I can tell you this man I am talking about. This is the one we all need more now than ever before. Those that have ears to hear let them hear what the spirit is saying to the church. I don't have a building to go in and write, but in my house. I am saying like Paul. I am writing with my own hadn't and if my hand give out, I will let someone else write it. I will sign it with my own hand. This I must do and I am just like Jonas, I didn't obey at first, now I am writing in a hurry. I got to tell this, I was supposed to write this in 1989, but I didn't. It is troubling my mind. I got to tell every man, woman, boy, and girl about this. In the book of Joel, said, first chapter and second verse said, Hear this ye old men and give ear all ye inhabitants of the land, hath this been in your days, or even in the days of your father's tell your children of it and let your children tell their children and let their children tell another generation. That which the palmer worn hath left, hath the locust eaten, and that which the locust hath left, hath the canker worm eaten and that which the canker worm hath left, hath the caterpillar eaten, awake, ye drunkards, and weep and howl. All ye drinkers of wine because of the new wine for it are cut off from your mouth. The new wine is the Holy Ghost. People want to give upon you. He said in his word, I am married to the back slider, but he said, I will give you a written divorce, that means he don't want you anymore. God is tired of fattening frogs for snakes for he said, you are with me or you are lost, so lets hold on to the one that left he want leave you, he will be with you to the grave, in the grave. So have he been, so will he do now. Hold on to him, Jesus is love. He gets tired too. He is a consuming fire (Hebrews 12:28). Wherefore, we receive a kingdom which can not be moved, let us have grace, where by we may serve God, acceptable with reverence and godly fear. For God is a consuming fire, Paul said (Romans 12:1). I beseech you brethren by the mercies of God that ye present your bodies a living sacrifice halt. Acceptable unto God, which is your reasonable service, and be not conformed to this world, but be ye transformed by the renewing of your mind that ye may prove what is that good and acceptable and perfect will of God, Paul said. I beg you, don't do like I did, Paul said. When I was on my way to Damascus about noon, suddenly there shone from Heaven a great light round about me and I fell unto the ground and heard a voice saying unto me, Saul, Saul, Why persecute thou me? And I answered, who art thou Lord? And he said unto me, I am Jesus of Nazareth, whim thou persecute and they that were with me saw, indeed the light and were afraid; but they heard not the voice of him that spoke to me and said, What shall I do Lord? And the Lord said unto me, Arise and go into Damascus and there it shall be told thee of all things which are appointed for thee to do, and when I could not see for the glory of that light, being led by the hand of them that were with me. I came into Damascus and one Ananias a devout man according to the law, having a good report of all the Jews which dealt there, came unto me, and stood and said unto me, brother Saul, receive thy sight, and the same hour I looked up upon him. Paul could see again (Acts 16) and why tarries thou? Arise and be baptized and wash away thy sins.

Calling on the name of the Lord (Acts 26:14). When we were all fallen to the earth, I heard a voice speaking unto me, and saying in Hebrew tongue, Saul, Saul, why persecute thou me? It is hard for thee to kick against the pricks. So Paul is saying don't try it. It doesn't work and we need someone to teach us what we should do and make God has someone to do so. God sends his preachers to teach and to warn us from the evil things of this world. Paul said, I tried killing God's people. I got myself in a mess. When we think we can go and do what we want to do, we are making a mistake and a bad one. God has an all seeing eye and he sees everything that we do. He hears everything we say. You can hide from man, but not from God. So if you don't know this, then you need to ask someone. This is some of our problem. We don't know and won't ask anyone. When Paul was blinded, then he wanted to know. What shall we do? Don't wait until you can't see. God don't have to give you your sight back. This is just like waiting until you are on your death bed to ask for forgiveness. God can do this, but why wait? That is to close of a call, why do so? God is God. He can do in the days of thy youth. While the evil times are not present. Don't treat your soul like that. Don't gamble with your soul, because that is all you have. The Bible said, what does it profit a man to gain the whole world and lose his own soul? (Matthew 16:26) What will you give for exchange for your soul? God wants us to prosper as our souls prosper. If we live right we can ask for what we want, not only for what we need. Psalms 23:1 says, The Lord is my Shepherd, I shall not want; He makes me to lie down in green pastures, and he leaded me beside still waters. God made the waters stand still for the children of Israel to pass through to dry land. He restored my soul. When my faith gets a little shaky, he restores me. He leaded me in the paths of righteousness for his name sake. When I wanted to go a little out of the word, he brought me back to use me for his servant. Yea, though I walk through the valley of the shadow of death, I will fear no evil, for thy art with me, thy rod and thy staff, they comfort me. Thy rod sometime hit hard, but thy staff holds me up. It doesn't let me fall. Thou prepare a table before me, in the presence of my enemies. God lets my enemies see me prosper in every way. Your enemies help you to grow. If you stay in good ground, you can keep your enemy on a wonder. So you don't have to worry about them while you are prospering. God is anoints my head with oil, my cup rennet over. Surely goodness and mercy shall follow me the days of my life; now if goodness and mercy is going to follow me all the days of my life as long as I live, that is good enough for me and I will dwell in the house of the Lord forever. When I am in the house with my father, I don't have to worry anymore about anything. If God be your shepherd, you don't have to stoop to the devil for anything he said. (Psalms 24:1) The earth is the Lord's and the fullness thereof. The world and they that dwell there in. If you accept Jesus, you have all you need. Jesus have saving in his hand and he have healing in his hand and he have keeping power in his hand. He will be everything to you that you need. Give God a chance. You don't have to look any further. Jesus is the closest one to you. Reach out and touch him. He get lives, he will live in you if you let him. Jesus said, I am the bread of life, and then said, they unto him Lord, evermore give us this bread.

Jesus said unto them, I am the bread of life, he that cometh to me shall never hunger, and he that believeth in me shall never thirst, but I say unto you, that ye also have seen me and believe not all that the father giveth shall come to me, and him that cometh to me I will in no wise cast out. For I cam down from Heaven not to do my own will, but the will of him that sent me. This is the father's will, which hath sent me, that of which he hath given me, I should lose nothing, but I should raise it up again at the last day. This is the will of him that sent me. That everyone, which seethe the son and believeth on him, may have everlasting life. I will raise him up at the last day (John 6:44). Jesus said. No man can come to me except by the father which hath sent me. Draw him and I will raise him up at the last day, God raised Jesus from the dead. Jesus will raise us from the dead spiritually and physically too. We will need to be raised and we will have to have a home, but it is our choice. Which one will we choose, Heaven or will we choose Hell? Choose this day that ye shall serve. It came to pass that as they went I a certain man said unto him, Lord, I will follow thee whosesoever thou guest and Jesus said unto him, Foxes have holes, and birds of the air have nests, but the son of man hath no where to lay his head. Go it is time to tell the truth and he said unto another, follow me, but he said, Lord, suffer me first to go and bury my father; Jesus said unto him, Let the dead bury their dead, but go thou and preach the kingdom of God, and another said, Lord, I will follow thee, but let me first bid them farewell, which are at home at my house, and Jesus said unto him, no man having put his hand to the plow and looking back is not fit for the kingdom of God. This is the problem today, we don't put God first. We bring him in later when we get into trouble. We want God to come in a hurry. Everyone is still trying to make an excuse when Jesus told us he took them to the cross. So don't look for one, you can't hide behind what you don't know. Sometimes it is better not to know so much on your own. You will have time to do what the Lord Say do and there was a certain Jew named Apollo's born at Alexandria. An eloquent man and mighty in his scriptures, came to Ephesus. This man was instructed in the way of the Lord and being fervent in the spirit. He spoke and taught diligently the things of the Lord, knowing only the baptism of John. He taught what he knew, and began to speak boldly in the synagogue. When Aquila and Priscilla had heard, they took him unto them and expounded unto him the way of God more perfectly. If you use what you got, God will add to what you have, but if you don't use what you have, God will take that from you and give it to someone else. It doesn't take a whole lot of faith, just use what you got. Faith doesn't work if you don't put it to work. Moses, Peter, and Abraham didn't know they had so much until they used it. Why not try yours? Faith without work, will not work at all. I don't have enough of man's wisdom to tell you what the president can tell you about is going on in the world today, but I can tell you Jesus said in 1st Samuel 2:6, The Lord kills and makes it alive. He brings down to the grave and brings up. The Lord makes poor and makes them rich. He brings low and lifts up high. (Samuel 7:8). He rises up the poor out of the dust and lifts up the beggar from the dunghill to set them among the princes, and to make them inherit the throne of glory. The pillars of the earth are the Lord's and he hath set the world upon them.

He will keep the feet of his saints and the wicked shall be silent in darkness; for by strength shall no man prevail. This is not by faith strength, but by the power of God. We can't fight and we can't win, our arms are too short and our hands are too small and we are not strong enough. We put everything in God's hand and leave it along. The battle is not ours, it belongs to God. He can fight and win. So, if we are in Jesus, we are on the winning side (Hebrews 4:12). The word of God is sharper and quicker than any two-edged sword, piercing even to the diving as under of soul and spirit, and the joints and marrow and intents of the heart (Samuel 13). Neither is there any creature that is not manifest in his sight, but all things are naked and open unto his eyes of him with whom we have to do. Seeing then that we have a great high priest that is passed unto the heavens, Jesus the son of God. Let us hold fast our profession, for we have not a high priest, which can not be toughed with the feeling of our infirmities, but was in all points tempted like we are. Get without sin, let us therefore come boldly unto the throne of grace;

that we may obtain mercy and find grace to help in times of need (Hebrews 12:14). Follow peace with all men and holiness without which no man shall see the Lord. We have to love those regardless of whatever comes our way. We have to forgive and forget, and love everyone. Make peace, not break peace, Jesus said. My peace, I leave with you, if you don't have peace, you don't have power (Acts 1:8). Ye shall receive power after that the Holy Ghost will come unto you and ye shall be witness unto me both in Jerusalem and in Judaea and in Samaria and unto the utter most part of the earth. When he had spoken these things, while they beheld, he was taken up and a cloud received him out of their sight. While they looked steadfastly toward heaven as he went up, behold, two men stood by them in white apparel; which also said, ye men of Galilee, Why stand ye gazing up in to heaven. This same Jesus, who is taken up from you into heaven, shall also come in like manner as ye have seen him go in to heaven. So we need power to witnesses. We can't witness without the Holy Ghost. We first must receive before we can give. We know by the word, Jesus is coming back. We have got to have that same power that Jesus had to be caught up. According to the word of God to meet him in the air if you can't see what is going on. You need to go down to the potter's house (Jeremiah 18:1). The word of God, which came to Jeremiah from the Lord, saying, Arise and go down to the potter's house and there I will cause thee to hear my words, then I went down to the potter's house, behold, he wrought a work on the wheels and the vessel that he made of clay was marred in the hand of the potter's so he made it again.

Another vessel as seemed good to the potter's to make it. The word of the Lord came to me saying, O house of Israel cannot I do with you as this potter's smith the Lord? Behold, as the clay is in the potter's, so are ye in mine hand. O house of Israel at what instant I shall speak concerning a nation and a kingdom to pluck up and to pull down and destroy it. If that nation is against whom I have pronounced, turn from their evil, I will repent of the evil that I thought to do unto them and at what instant I shall speak concerning a nation and a kingdom to build and plant it. If it does evil in my sight, that it obeys not my voice, then I will repent of the good, where with I said I would benefit them. Now, therefore, go to the inhabitants of Jerusalem, saying thus, said the Lord, behold, I frame evil against you and devise against you.

Return ye now everyone from his evil ways, and make your ways and your doing good, and they said, there is no hope, but we will walk after our own devices, and we will do the imagination of his evil heart. We are in the hands of the Lord, what we need to ask God to work on us. Let him wake us up, shake us, makes us stir our own mind, and our hearts, and settle us, and then ask God to use us. Somebody wants to be made, but don't want the test, and that don't work. God don't make you stay in the mold, you make the choice whether you stay or not. If you don't like what or who you are, let God work on you. After all we belong to him (Ezekiel 18:4) said, all souls are mine, but the soul that sins shall die, and fear not them which kill the body, but are not able to kill the soul; rather fear him which is able to destroy both soul and body in hell.

Someone today is afraid to make a move because of man, it is better to obey God than man. Someone is waiting on mother, someone is waiting on daddy. Don't wait, time waits on no man. If you waiting on sister, she might not go, if you waiting on brother, he might not go, by this you can wait to late. Don't wait on your friends, Jesus is the best friend you can ever have. Those that have ears to hear, let them hear what the spirit is saying to the church. Don't turn a deaf ear to the word of God. We read about what God has already done, and he is the same God today, yesterday, and forever more (Hebrews 13:8). God don't change, man change. Jesus is the same man that can tell you when the weather is going to change, but no man can tell you when Jesus is going to come. That is why he said be ready, the Pharisees, also with the sad, Duchess came and tempting desired him that he would show them a sign from Heaven. He answered and said unto them, when it is evening, ye say it will be fair weather for the sky is red, and in the morning, it will be foul weather today, and for the sky is red and lowering. O, ye hypocrites, ye can discern the face to the sky, but can ye not discern the signs of the times. A wicked and adulterous generation, seek after a sign; and there shall be no sign given unto it, but the sign of the prophet Jonas, and he left them and departed, and now, we are looking for a sign, if you can't see the time is near, if you don't know, you better ask somebody. Most people are going to hell with their eyes wide open. Don't be like the rich man. He got in a mess, some said, I'd give my body to burn (1 Corinthians 13:1) said, though I speak with the tongue of men, and of angels, have no charity, I am becoming as sound brass or tinkling cymbal, and though I have the gift of prophecy and understand all mysteries, and all knowledge and though I have all faith, so that I could remove mountains, and have not charity. I am nothing and though I bestow all my goods to feed the poor and though I give my body to be burned, and have not charity, it profits me nothing, charity suffering long, and is kind. Charity envied not, charity vaunted not, itself is not puffed up. Both not behave itself, unseemly, keep not her own, is not easily provoked, think no evil. Rejoice not iniquity, but rejoice in the truth bearing all things, believing all things, hoping all things, enduring all things charity never failing, but whether there be prophecies. They shall fail, whether their be tongues, they shall cease, where there be knowledge, it shall vanish away; for we know in part, and we prophesy in part, but when that which is perfect is come, then that which is in part shall be done away.

When I was a childe, I spoke as a child, I understood as a child, I thought as a child, but when I became a man, I put away childish things. It is time to speak for yourself and speak the truth from your heart and not beating in the air. You are of age now, if you can read, and if you can hear, let your ears hear what the spirit is saying to the church. You are of age, speak now, it is your time. If you can see, tell someone else the truth, and as Jesus passed by, he saw a man born blind from his birth, and his disciples asked him, saying, Master, Who did sin, this man or his parents, that he was born blind? Jesus answered, neither hath this man sinned nor his parents, but the works of God should be made manifest in him. I must work the works of him that sent me, while it is day. The night cometh, when no man can work, as long as I am in the world. I am the light of the world, when he had thus spoken, he spat on the ground and made clay of the spit and he anointed the eyes of the blind man with the clay and said unto him, go wash in the pool of Siloam, which is by interpretation sent. He went his way therefore; and washed and came seeing (John 9-1:7). The neighbors therefore, and which before had seen him, that was blind, said is not this he that sat and begged; some said this is he, this man was saving I am he, but I am not blind anymore, I am he, but I am not begging anymore, because I got what I need. God gave me my eye sight. I am he and I know who gave me my eye sight, verse 16 said. Therefore, some of the Pharisees said this man is not of God because he kept not the Sabbath day, others said, how can a man do that is a sinner, do such miracles? There was a division among them. They said unto the blind man again, what safest thou of him that he hath opened thine eyes? He said, He is a prophet, but the Jews did not believe concerning him, that he had been blind and received his sight until they called the parents of him that had received his sight. They asked them, saying, is this your son, who ye say was born blind? How then doth he see? His parents answered them and said, we know that this is our son and that he was born blind, but by means he now sees, we know not, or who opened his eyes. We know now he is of age, ask him, he can speak for himself. If you have a mouth, you can speak for yourself. It doesn't make any different about your age. God can use the children also. When God was calling Samuel he was a child (Samuel 3:1). The child ministered unto the Lord before Eli and the word of the Lord was precious in those days. There was no open vision. Now the word of God is very plentiful. Catch on an hold on and speak your part and it came to pass at that time when Eli was laid down in his place, and his eyes began to way dim, that he could not see. This is the problem in this hour. So many have laid down and went to sleep and can't get a message from God. To help in this hour, someone is in a need today. Lets wake up an hear the word of God. That the Lord called Samuel and he answered, here am I, and he ran unto Eli and said here am I. For thou call me and he went, I called not, lie down again, and he went and laid down, and the Lord called yet again, Samuel, and Samuel arose and went to Eli and said here am I for thou did call me, and he answered, I called not my son. Lie down again now. Samuel did not yet know the Lord, neither was the word of the Lord yet revealed unto him, and the Lord called Samuel again the third time and he arose and went to Eli and said here am I for thou did call me and Eli perceived that the Lord called the child.

Therefore, Eli said unto Samuel, go lie down, and it shall be if he calls thee, that thou shall, say speak Lord for thy servant hears. So Samuel went and lay down in his place and the Lord came and stood and called as at other times. Samuel then answered, speak, for thy servant hears and the Lord said to Samuel, behold, I will do a thing in Israel, at which both thee ears of everyone that hears it shall tingle in that day. I will perform against Eli all things which I have spoken concerning his house when I begin. I will also make and end, for I have told him that I will judge his house for ever for the iniquity which he knows because his sons made themselves vile and he restrained them not. See God have already told us that sin is in the house, but again God choose to speak to Eli's son to let Eli know to clean up your house. I am warning you, I am doing it again, you know what is going on and keeping it inside. You have to speak up against wrong doing regardless of who it is and you can love to your own heart hurt. Sometimes our children can keep us from obeying God. Jesus said, have nothing before him. Tell you children the truth. If it hurt them, it will help them. Your children will love you for the truth in the long run because sooner or later someone will tell them the truth and make you look stupid. The word is uncovering sin. It will be uncovered. Eli lay down and went to sleep and lost track of what was going on in his house. This is the problem in this hour. Most people have did like wise. The Devil is calling our children and Jesus is calling too. We need to be able to tell them which one to answer to whether they here or not. We are supposed to stay awake and sober, for our children so they can call on us. When they are in need Deuteronomy 28 explain this matter? It shall come to pass, if thou shalt hearken diligently unto the voice of the Lord thy God, to observe and to do all his commandments which I have commended thee this day, thy Lord thy God will set thee on high above all nations of the earth, and all these blessings shall come onto thee and over take thee if thou shall hearken unto the voice of the Lord thy God. Blessed shall thou be in the city and blessed shall thou be in the field. Blessed shall be the fruit of thy body and the fruit of thy ground and the fruit of thy cattle's. The increase of thy kind and the flocks of thy sheep, blessed shall be thy basket, and thy store. Blessed shall thy be when thou come in and blessed shall thy be when thou guest out, the Lord shall cause thine enemies to rise up against thee to be smitten before thy face. They shall come out against thee one way, and flee before thee seven ways. The Lord shall command the blessing upon thee in thy storehouse; and all that thou set test thine hand unto do and he shall bless thee in the land which the Lord thy God given thee. The Lord shall establish the and holy people unto himself as he hath sworn unto thee. If thou shall keep the commandments of the Lord thy God and walking his ways and all peoples of the earth shall see, that thou art called by the name of the Lord, and they shall be afraid of thee, and the Lord make thee plenteous in goods, in fruit of thy body, and in the fruit of thy cattle's, and in the fruit of thy ground, in the land which the Lord swear unto thy fathers to give thee. The Lord shall open unto thee his good treasure, the heaven to give the rain unto thy land in his season and to bless all the work of thine hand, and thou shall lend unto many nations, and thou shall not borrow (Deuteronomy 28-1:14). The Lord shall make you the head and not the tail, and thou shall be above only.

And thou shall not be beneath. If that thou hearken unto the commandments of the Lord thy God, which command thee, this day to observe and do them. Thou shall not go aside from any of the words which I command thee this day to the right hand or to the left, to go after other Gods. ; and to serve them. We have always heard how God would bless us, but we need to know that God will curse some too. God will do all he said that he would. Every time something bad happens, it is not always the Devil. The Devil can't do no more that God allow him to do. I will tell you Verse 14 said, But it come to pass if thou will not hearken unto the voice of the Lord thy God, to observe to do all his commandments and his statutes, which command thee this day, that all these curses shall come up on thee and overtake thee, cursed shall thou be in the city and cursed shall thou be in the field; cursed shall thy basket and thy store, cursed shall be the fruit of thy body, and the fruit of thy land, thy increase of thy kind and the flocks of thy sheep. Cursed shall thou be when thou come in and cursed shall thou be when thou goes out; the Lord shall send upon thee cursing vexation and rebuke in all that, thou, set test thine hand unto for to do until thou be destroyed and until thou perish quickly because of the sickness of thy doings, where by thou hast forsaken me. The Lord shall make pestilence; cleave unto thee, until he has consumed thee from off the land. Which thou go to possess it. The Lord shall smite thee with a consumption and with a fever and with inflammation and with an extreme burning and with the sword, and with blasting and with mildew, and they shall pursue the until thou perish and thy heaven that is over thy head shall be brass and the earth that is under thee shall be iron. The Lord shall make the rain of thy land powder and dust from heaven shall it come down up on thee, until thou be destroyed. The Lord shall cause thee to be smitten before thine enemies;

thou shall go out one way against them and flee seven ways before them and shall be removed unto all the kingdoms of the earth. When things are not going on well with us, we ought to just say, I started this mess, I am not going to fault God, and just say, Lord it is my fault, it is me that is in a need Lord. I need you, and say Lord bring me out, and God will receive you back, he is a God with more than a 2nd chance. God wants to send healing for the backslider (Isaiah 57:18). The Lord I have seen his ways and will heal him. I will lead him also and restore comfort unto him, and to his mourners, I will create the fruit of the lips and to him that is near, said the Lord and I will heal him. The wicked are like the troubled sea when it cannot rest, whose waters cast up mire and dirt. There is no peace said my God. To the wicked this said (Isaiah 58:1). Cry loud and spare not, lift up thy voice like a trumpet and show my people their transgressions and the house of Jacob their sins. Yet they seek me daily, and delight to know my ways and as a nation that did righteousness and forsake not the ordinance of their God. They ask of me the ordinances of Justice. They take delight in approaching to God. Wherefore, have we fasted said they and thou sees not wherefore, have we afflicted our soul and thou takes no knowledge? Behold, in the day of your fast ye find pleasure and exact all your labors, behold, ye fast for strife, and debate, and to smite with the fist of wickedness; ye shall not fast as ye do this day, to make your voice be heard on high, is it such a fast that I have chosen? A day for a man to afflict his soul? Is it to bow down his head as a bullish and to spread sack cloth? Ashes under him, wilt thou call this a fast; and an acceptable day to the Lord; is not this fast that I have chosen? To lose the bands of wickedness to undo the heavy burdens, and to let the opposed go free, and that ye break every yoke, is it not to daily bread to the hungry and that thou shall bring the poor that are cast out to thy house? When thou see the naked, that thou cover him and that thou hide not thy self from my own flesh? Then shall thy light break forth as a morning and thine health shall spring forth speedily and thy righteousness shall go before thee, the glory of the Lord shall be thy reward.

They shalt thou call and the Lord shall answer. Thou shall cry and he shall say, Here I am if hot take away from the midst of thee the yoke, the putting forth of the finger, and speaking vanity and if thou draw out thy soul tithe hungry and satisfy the afflicted soul, then shall thy light rise in obscurity and the darkness, be as the noon day, and the Lord shall guide thee continually, and satisfy thy soul in drought, and make fat thy bones and thou shall be like a watered garden, and like a spring of water whose water fail not. And they that shall be of thee shall build the old waste places. Thou shall raise up the foundations of many generations and thy shall be call the repairer of the breach, the restorer of paths to dwell in (Isaiah 59:1) said this, Behold, the Lord's hand is not shortened, that it cannot save, neither his ear heavy, that it cannot hear, but your iniquities have separated between you and your God, and your sins have hid his face from you, that he will not hear, for your hands are defiled with blood and your fingers with iniquity; your lips have spoken lies, your tongues hath muttered perverseness, none called for justice, nor any plead for thy truth. They trust in vanity and speak lies. They conceive mischief, and bring forth iniquity, so when we are separated from god. That means we are not with him anymore, we are calling, but we are separated from him, so we have to get back in him to be blessed. We fast, we pray and it doesn't seem like we are getting through to God. We are not together (John 15:1) said, I am the true vine, and my father is the husband, every branch in me that bears not fruit, take it away and every branch that bears fruit, he prunes it. That it may bring forth more fruit. Now ye are clean through the word which I have spoken Jesus said unto us. Abide in me, and I in you as the branch cannot bear fruit of itself, except ye abide in me, I am the vine ye are the branches. He that abide in me, and I am him, the same bring forth much fruit. For without me ye can do nothing, if a man abide not in me he is cast forth as a branch, and is withered, and a man gather them, and cast them into the fire, and they are burned. If ye abide in me and my word abides in you, you shall ask what ye will, and it shall be done unto you. Sometimes we need to check ourselves and see if we are still connected to Jesus. When we cannot get thing to go right, fault is in us, when they were trying to find fault in Jesus, they always said, I cannot find no fault in him (Luke 22:1). After the whole multitude of them, arose, and led him unto palate, and they began to accuse him, saying, we found this fellow preventing the nation and forbidding giving tribute to Caesar, saying that he, himself is Christ, a king, and palate ask him saying, Art thou the king of the Jews? And he answered him and said, Thou say it, then said the palate, to the chief of priests and to the people, I find no fault in this man, and they were the more fierce, saying he stirred up the people. Teaching throughout all Jewry beginning from Galilee to this place.

When palate heard of Galilee, he asked whether he Wawa's a Galician and as soon as he knew that he belonged unto Herds jurisdiction he sent him to Herod, who himself also was at Jerusalem at that time, and when Herod saw Jesus, he was exceedingly glad; for he was detour to see him of a long season because he had heard many things of him, and he hoped to have seen some. Miracle done by him, then he questioned with him in many words, but he answered him nothing. This is a problem today. We want to ask so many questions (John 2:5) Jesus mother said unto the servant, what so ever he said unto you, do it. And there set there six water pots of the Jews containing 2 or 3 firkins a piece. Jesus said unto them, fill the water pots with water, and they filled them up to the brim and he said unto them draw out now, and bear unto governor of the feast, and they bare it. When the rulers of the feast had tasted the water that was made of wine and knew to whence it was, but the servants which drew the water knew. The governor of the feast called the bridegroom an d said unto him, Every man at the beginning doth set forth good wine, and when men have well drunk, then that which is worse, but thou hast kept the good wine until now, and Jesus have better things for us now to get them. Just get in the word of god. (1 Cor. 2:9) said, but it is so written, eyes hath not seen, nor ears have heard, neither have entered unto the heart of man, the things which God hath prepared for them that love him. God hath revealed them unto us by his spirit for the spirit searches all things, yea, the deep things of god (2 Cor. -17) said, therefore, if any man be in Christ, he is a new creature, old things are have passed away, and all things are new, and all things are of God. Who hath reconciled us to himself by Jesus Christ, and hath given to us the ministry of reconciliation, to with that God was in Christ reconciling the word unto him. Not imputing their trespasses unto them and hath committed unto us the word of reconciliation. God is saying, if you want to know the hidden things of him, you have to get in him. Everything is not written in the book, something's are being revealed to God's people. If you are not in him, you are on the outside looking in. You can't see it, and you can't hear it. And you can't feel it in your heart. You desire to know, but you can't if God called you to preach. He gives the message on what to preach. When we get all the way back in him, and not close to him (John 10:14) I am the good shepherd and know my sheep, and I am known of mine, as the father knows me, even so I know the father, and I lay down my life for the sheep and other sheep. I have which are not o f this fold them also. I must bring and they shall hear my voice, and there shall be one fold and one shepherd too. So if you are not in Jesus, and he is not in you, you are not of him, and know not him and can not hear his voice, he said, my sheep know my voice, and a strange they want follow (John 10:4) and when he put forth his own sheep, he went before them and the sheep followed him, foot they know his voice. If you have a father a natural father you live with him everyday. When you hear his voice, you know his voice from anyone else. It is something about that voice that is different for anyone else's. That makes a connection to your father. He can call you and you will answer him, if not, you will receive a punishment and if you don't answer your heavenly father, you will receive a greater punishment and if he call you to preach, he didn't say they would hear, he said there would come a day when they would not endure sound doctrine (Timothy 4:1) Paul was instructing Timothy, I charge thee, therefore before God, and the Lord Jesus Christ who shall judge the quick and the dead at his appearing and his kingdom. Preach the word; be instant in season and out of season; reprove, rebuke, exhort with all longsuffering and doctrine.

For the time will come when they will not endure sound doctrine, but after their own lusts shall they heal to themselves. Teachers have itching ears and they shall turn away their ears from the truth and shall be turned unto fables, but watch thou in all things, endure affliction, do the work of an evangelist. Make full proof of thy ministry for I am now ready to be offered and the time of y departure is at hand. I have fought a good fight, I have finished my course, I have kept the faith, hence forth there is laid up for me a crow o righteousness, which the Lord, the righteous judge shall give me, at that day and not to me only, but unto all them also that love his appearing, you have to love hi at his coming and welcome him to get a crow of life. You have to love before he gets here. Paul taught Timothy, telling him, I did this, you can do it also, you can't get upset when they want hear the word. The word didn't say that they would hear, preach it, if they hear, preach it, if they forbear. Somebody didn't hear in the older days. They will not hear now. Just tell it, when Noah was preaching they didn't hear, he didn't stop. When Noah was warning the people (Genesis 7:1). And the Lord said unto Noah, come thou and all thy house in to the Ark for thy have seen righteousness before me in this generation, of every clean beast, thou shall take to thee by sevens. The male and his female and of beasts, that are not clean by two. The male and his female, to keep seed alive upon the face of all the earth, for yet seven days, and I will cause it to rain upon the earth forty days, and forty nights, and every living substance that I have made will I destroy from off the face of the earth. Noah did according unto all that the Lord commanded him, and he was six hundred years old when the flood of waters was upon the earth. Noah went in and his sons and his wife, and his son's wife with him into the Ark because of the waters of the flood, of clean beasts, and of beasts that are not clean and of fowls and of everything that crept upon the earth. There went in two and two unto the Ark. The male and female, as God had commanded Noah, and it came to pass after seven days, that the waters of the flood were upon the earth, in the sit hundredth year of Noah's life, in the second month, the seventeenth day of the month, the same day were all the fountains of the great deep broken up, and the windows of heaven were opened. The rain was upon the earth forty days and forty nights in the same day entered Noah and Shem, and Ham, and Japheth, the sons of Noah, and

Noah's wife and three wives of his sons with them. I am the Ark they and every beast after his kind and every creeping thing that crept upon the earth after his kind and every fowl after his kind, every bird of every sort. Then went in unto Noah, into the Ark. Two and two, of flesh where in is the breath of life, and they that went in, went in male and female of all flesh, as God had commanded him, and the Lord shut him in, and the flood was for forty days upon the earth, and the waters increase, and bare up the Ark and it was lifted up above earth. The waters prevailed and increased greatly upon the earth and the Ark went upon the face of the waters and the waters prevailed exceedingly upon the earth and all the high hills that were under the whole heaven, were covered.

Fifteen cubits upward did the waters prevail and the mountains were covered and al flesh died that moved peon the earth, both of fowl and of cattle and of beast and every creeping thing that crept upon the earth, and every man; all in whose no strips was the breath of life of all that was in the dry land died and every living substance was destroyed which was upon the face of the ground, both man and cattle's and the creeping things and the fowl of the heaven. They were destroyed from the earth and Noah only remained alive and they that were with him in the Ark and the waters prevailed upon the earth a hundred and fifty days (Genesis 7:24). Noah could have given up, but he believed God, what will God have to do for you to believe the word of God? These things going on now, this is not the first time this has happened. Noah told them that it was going to rain, they didn't believe him, and the same thing people now are still mocking after people that try to warn them, the Bible said in the book, Noah was a righteousness man who lived during a time of evil and corruption (6:8). God instructed Noah to build a Ark, which God used to save a small number of people and animals and he destroyed others in the flood, because he obeyed God. So, as it was in the day of Noah, so shall it be when the son of man comes again. Things are so crocket now. It will take God to straighten it out. So if you want to be straighten out, get in the word of God, and let him do it. It is time to do like Saul, get straight and come back and beg someone else to come, stop killing, and tell them how to get life back in them. When God told Ezekiel to go down I the valley and preach to the dry bones, they were dead, and dry, but God told Ezekiel to go preach to them. They came up out of the grave. You can come up too (Ezekiel 37:1) These are the words of the Lord, the hand of the Lord was upon me, and carried me out in the spirit of the Lord, and set me down in the mist of the valley, which was full of bones, and caused me to pass by them round about; and behold, there were very many in the open valley and they were very dry, and he said unto me, Son of man, can these bones live? And I answered, O, Lord God, thou know. Again, he said unto me, prophesy upon these bones, and say unto them, O ye, dry bones, hear the word of the Lord, thus said the Lord God, unto these bones; Behold, I will cause breath to enter into you and ye shall live and I will lay sinews upon you, and will bring up flesh upon you and cover you with skin, and put breath in you, and ye shall live and ye shall know that I am the Lord, so I prophesied as I was commanded and as I prophesied, there was a noise and behold a shaking, and the bone came together, bone to his bone and when I beheld, lo, the sinews and the flesh came upon them but there was no breath in them, then said, he unto me prophesy unto the wind, prophesy, son of man, and say to the wind, thus said the Lord God, come from four winds, O, breath and breathe upon these slain, that they may live. So I prophesied, as he commanded me and the breath came into them and they lived, and stood up upon there feet. An exceedingly great army, this is what God is speaking to us today. For us to get together and then we will see God move. Every preacher, deacon, mother, and all members, get together and come alive and then stand on your feet, gain strength and then you can hold on when you know your job. Do it and you will get paid for your work. He also knows your heart. What you do come from within your heart, if not, it has not affect.

WORK YOUR PROBLEMS OUT WITH GOD

Work out your own soul salvation with trembling fear. To work it out, it has to be in you. It is time to put our work here our words are in faith. We have a wall built that must come down. It will come down only by fasting and praying. In the book of Joshua 5:13, and it came to pass when Joshua was by Jericho that he lifted up his eyes and looked and behold, there stood a man over against him with his sword drawn in his hand and Joshua went to him and said unto him, Art thou for us? Or for our adversaries? And he said, nay, but as captain of the host of the Lord, am I now. Come, and Joshua fell on his face to the earth, and did worship and said unto him, what smith my Lord unto his servant? And the captain of the Lord's host said unto Joshua, Loose thy shoes from off thy foot; for the place where on you stand is holy, and Joshua did so (Joshua (6). Now Jericho was straightly shut up because of the children of Israel; none went out and none came in and the Lord said unto Joshua, See I have given into thine hand Jericho and the king there of and mighty men of Velour and ye shall compass the city once, thus shall thou do six days, and seven priests shall bear before the Ark seven trumpets of Rams horns, and when ye hear the sound of the trumpet, all the people shall shout with a great shout and the wall of the city shall fall down flat and the people shall ascend up every man straight before him, and Joshua, the son of nun called the priests, and said unto them, Take up the Ark of the covenant, and let seven priests bear seven trumpets of Rams horns before the Ark of the Lord and this is what we have to do today. Start marching so the wall can come down between us. There are walls between our preachers, deacons, walls in our church, and in our homes. Let's start marching it is time to bring down the walls of Satan. He has gotten to big for things to last, and together we can stand, but divided we will fall. Let's shout the Devil kingdom down.

Let us pray it down, let us preach it down, let us weigh it down, but we have to be together, if we don't always agree, Isaiah 1:18 said, Come now, and let us reason together, smith the Lord, though your sins may be as scarlet, they shall be as white as snow; though they be red like crimson, they shall be as wool, if ye be willing and obedient, ye shall eat the good of the land, but if ye refuse and rebel, ye shall be devoured with the sword; for the mouth of the Lord hath spoken it. How does a faithful city become a harlot? It is full of judgment; righteousness lodged in it, but now murderers. Thy silver has become dross, thy wine mixed with water, they princes are rebellious, and companions of thieves. Everyone love gifts and follow after rewards. They judge not the fatherless, neither doth the cause of widow come unto them, therefore smith the Lord, the Lord of hosts, the mighty one of Israel, Ah, I will ease me of mine adversaries, and avenge me of my enemies, and I will turn my hand upon thee and purely purge away thy dross and take away all thy sin; and I will restore thy judges as at the first, and thy counselors as at the beginning; Afterward thou shall be called, the city of righteousness, the faithful city (Isaiah 59:1). Behold, the Lord hand is not shortened that it can not save, neither his ear heavy, that it cannot hear, but your iniquities have separated you from God and your sins have hid his face from you that he will not hear; for your hands are defiled with blood, and your fingers with iniquity; your lips have spoken lies, your tongue hath muttered perverseness, none called for justice, nor any pleaded for truth. They trust in your vanity, and speak lies; they conceive mischief and bring forth iniquity. They hatch cockatrice eggs, and weave the spider's web. He that eats of their eggs shall die and that which is crushed, will break out into a viper. Their webs shall thy cover themselves with their works. Their works are works of iniquity and the act of violence is in their hands. Their feet run to evil and they make haste to shed innocent blood. Their thoughts are thoughts of iniquity; wasting and destruction are in their paths. The way of peace they know not; and there is no judgment in there goings. They have made their crooked paths who so ever goes there shall know no peace; therefore, is judgment far from us, neither doth justice overtake us, we wait for the light, but behold, obscurity, for brightness, but we walk in darkness, we grope for the wall like the blind, and we grope as if we had no eyes, we stumble at noon day, as in the night, we are in desolate places as dead men, we roar all like bears, and mourn sore like doves. We look for judgment, but there is none, for salvation, but it is far off from us, for our transgressions are multiplied before thee and our sins testify against us. For our transgressions are with us, and as for our iniquities, we know them, in transgression and lying against the Lord and departing away from our God. Speaking oppression and revolt, conceiving and uttering from the heart words of falsehood and judgment is turned away backward, and justice standout far off. For truth is fallen in the streets and equity cannot enter. Yea truth fallen and he that depart from evil, makes himself prey and the Lord saw it and it displeased him that there was no judgment, and he saw that there was no man, and wondered that there was no intercessor; Therefore, his arm sustained him, for he put on righteousness, it breast plate, and a helmet of salvation upon his head and he put on the garments of vengeance for clothing, and was clad with zeal as a cloak, according to their deeds.

He will repay, fury to his adversaries, recompense to his enemies, to the islands, he will repay recompense, so shall they fear the name of the Lord. From the west and his glory from the rising of the sun, when the enemy shall come in like a flood. The spirit of the Lord shall life up a standard against him. (Isaiah 59:16) and the redeemer shall come to Zion and unto them that turn from transgression in Jacob said the Lord and as for me, this is my covenant with them, said the Lord. My spirit that is upon thee and my words, which I have put in thy mouth, shall not depart out of thy mouth, nor out of the mouth of thy seed, said the Lord. From hence, forth and forever, if we obey the word, we want have to want for any good things. We will be blessed in our going, we will be blessed in our coming, our children will be blessed, and their children. When we have everything going wrong, we are serving other Gods (Matthew 4:7), Jesus said unto him, talking to Satan, It is written again, thou shall not tempt the Lord, thy God; again the devil took him up into an exceeding high mountain, and showed him all the kingdoms of the world, and the glory of them, and said unto him, All these things will I give thee if thou will fall down and worship me, then said Jesus unto him, germ thee hence, Satan for it is written thou shall worship the Lord thy God and him only shall thou serve. God said, I am a jealous God, in the books of Exodus 20:1, and God spoke all these words saying, I am the Lord thy God, which have brought thee out of the Land of Egypt, out of the house of bondage. Thou shall have no other Gods before me. Thou shall not make unto thee my graven image, or any likeness of anything that is in heaven above, if that is in the earth beneath, or that is in the water under the earth, thou shall not bow down thyself to them, nor serve them, for I the Lord thy God, I am a jealous God. Visiting the iniquity of the fathers upon the children unto the third and fourth generation of them that hate me, and showing mercy unto thousands of them that love me and keep my commandments. Thou shall not take the name of the Lord thy God in vain, for the Lord will not hold him guiltless, that take his name in vain. God will not share us with the devil, he takes all of us, or none at all. He wants all of our body, mind, body, and soul. He doesn't want a part-time lover, if not all of you, all your work is in vain (Psalms 127:1). Except the Lord build the house, they labor in vain that build it. Except the Lord keep the city, the watchman wakes but in vain, it is vain for you to rise up early, to sit up late, and to eat bread of sorrows, for so he gives his beloved sleep. You don't have to trouble over work your mind, its not going profit you anything or anyone else (Revelation 2:5), said, Remember, therefore, from whence thou art fallen, and repent, and do thy first works, over or else I will come unto thee quickly and will remove thy candlestick our of his place, except tour repent, but this thou hast that thou hates the deed of the Nicolaitans, which also I hate he that hath an ear, let him hear what the spirit said unto the churches, to him that overcomes, and there is not middle class, and there is no low class, either, in Jesus. He said my people, all souls are mine, but that soul that sins shall die (Ezekiel 18:4), said, Behold all souls are mine as the soul of the father. So also the soul of the son is mine, the soul that sins it shall die.

Why would you have to be labored? You don't have anything to save but your soul, or you don't have anything to lose but your soul (Matthew 16:26), said, for what is a man to profit, if he shall gain the whole world, and lose his own soul? Or what shall a man give in exchange for his soul? Think about this one when a rich man dies, he is just as broke as the poor man in the poor house. We don't own anything but our own soul. I will say like Paul, I beg you to wake up. We are sleeping in dangerous times (Philippians 2:25), said, Fulfill ye my joy, that ye be like minded, having the same love being of one accord, of one mind, let nothing be done through strife of vain glory, but in lowliness of mind. Let us esteem other better than you. Look not every man on his own thing, but every man also on the things of others. Let this mind be in you, which was also in Christ Jesus. Who being in the form of God, thought it not robbery to be equal with God, but made himself of no pupation, and took him the form of a servant and was made in the like of man. He humbled himself and became obedient unto death, even the death of the cross. Wherefore, God also hath highly exalted him and given him a name which is above every name that at that name of Jesus, every knee shall bow of things in heaven and things in earth, and things under the earth, and that every tongue should confess, that Jesus Christ is Lord, to the glory of the God the father, for my beloved, have always obeyed not as in my present only, but now much mine in my absence, work out your own soul salvation with fear and trembling; for it is God which works in both to will and to do of his good pleasure. Do all things without murmuring and disputing, that ye maybe blameless, and harmless as doves. Go forth as sheep in the midst of wolves. Be ye there fore wise as serpents and harmless as doves, but aware of men for they will deliver you up to the councils and they will scourge you in their synagogues and ye shall be brought before governors and kings for my name sake for a testimony against them and the Gentiles but when they deliver you up take no thought how or what ye shall speak for it shall be given in that same hour what ye shall speak. When you are willing to speak it is not hard to do. Let God speak through you. He will give you his word so you don't have to think what I will say. When you study long, you study wrong and to your words don't mean anything. If God send you, you don't have to be afraid to go (Proverbs 3:6). In all ways acknowledge him and he shall direct thy paths. Be not wise in thine own eyes, fear the Lord, and depart from evil and it shall be healthy to thy navel and marrow to thy bones. We don't have the answer until God speaks (Isaiah 55:8) said these words, for my thoughts are not your thoughts, neither are your ways my ways, said the Lord. For as heavens are higher than the earth, so are my ways higher than your way and my thoughts than your thoughts. For as the rain comes down, and returns not there, but waters to the earth, and makes it bring forth and bud, that it may give seed to the sower, and bread to the eater, so shall my word be that goes forth out of my mouth, it shall not return unto me void, but it shall accomplish that which I please, and it shall prosper in the things where I sent it. Sometimes we can say one thing and do something else. The mind of man will change (James 1:8) said, 8A double minded man is unstable in all his ways. We can lose our minds trying to figure out the mind of Jesus.

Just whatever he says does, just do that, (2 Timothy 1:7) said these words, 7For God hath not given us the spirit of fear; but of power, and of love, and of a sound mind. 8Be not thou therefore ashamed of the testimony of our Lord, nor of me his prisoner: but be thou partaker of the afflictions of the gospel according to the power of God; 9Who hath saved us, and called us with an holy calling, not according to our works, but according to his own purpose and grace, which was given us in Christ Jesus before the world began; which was, we loved him, because he first loved us, if a man say, I love God, and hates his brother, he is a liar. For he that loves not his brother whom he has seen, how can he love God, whom he has not seen? This commandment we have from him, that he, who loves God, loves his brother also. We need to ask ourselves a question, do I love anybody and go from there. Check your own life and see, because if you can't love anyone, something is wrong somewhere. If you be honest with yourself, you can be honest with everyone else. We are not to lie to our fellow man because a lie will come out from under the cover. Like it did in (Acts 5: 1-11), But a certain man named Ananias, with Sapphire his wife, sold a possession, 2And kept back part of the price, his wife also being privy to it, and brought a certain part, and laid it at the apostles' feet. 3But Peter said, Ananias, why hath Satan filled thine heart to lie to the Holy Ghost, and to keep back part of the price of the land? 4Whiles it remained, was it not thine own? And after it was sold, was it not in thane own power? Why hast thou conceived this thing in thane heart? Thou hast not lied unto men, but unto God. 5And Ananias hearing these words fell down, and gave up the ghost: and great fear came on all them that heard these things. 6And the young men arose, wound him up, and carried him out, and buried him. 7And it was about the space of three hours after, when his wife, not knowing what was done, came in. 8And Peter answered unto her, Tell me whether ye sold the land for so much? And she said, yea, for so much. 9Then Peter said unto her, How is it that ye have agreed together to tempt the Spirit of the Lord? Behold, the feet of them which have buried thy husband are at the door, and shall carry thee out. 10Then fell her down straightway at his feet, and yielded up the ghost: and the young men came in, and found her dead and, carrying her forth, buried her by her husband. 11And great fear came upon all the church, and upon as many as heard these things. Today when the people of God get their message, God is speaking, Why don't you hear the word of the God, When will you hear? When will you fear? God is speaking everyday, every hour. Lying is a deadly weapon, but the truth will stand. God's word is the truth and it will stand when the world is on fire. Those that have ears to hear, let them hear what the sprit is saying to the church. Lying will kill you fast, quick, and in a hurry. Make a change if you are going around lying. Stop telling lies because the ungodly shall not stand in the judgment, nor shall the sinners in the congregation of the righteous, for the Lord knows the way of the righteous, but the way of the ungodly shall perish. We know everything is going down, but the word of God. If you can see, you know it is going down right now.

Man wants to make their own God, and have forgotten about the real God. (Exodus 32:24) said, And when the people saw that Moses delayed to come down out of the mount, the people gathered themselves together unto Aaron, and said unto him, Up, make us gods, which shall go before us; for as for this Moses, the man that brought us up out of the land of Egypt, we woot not what is become of him. 2And Aaron said unto them, Break off the golden earrings, which are in the ears of your wives, of your sons, and of your daughters, and bring them unto me. 3And all the people brake off the golden earrings which were in their ears, and brought them unto Aaron. 4And he received them at their hand, and fashioned it with a graving tool, after he had made it a molten calf: and they said, these be thy gods, O Israel, which brought thee up out of the land of Egypt. 5And when Aaron saw it, he built an altar before it; and Aaron made proclamation, and said, to morrow is a feast to the LORD. 6And they rose up early on the morrow, and offered burnt offerings, and brought peace offerings; and the people sat down to eat and to drink, and rose up to play. 7And the LORD said unto Moses, Go, get thee down; for thy people, which thou brightest out of the land of Egypt, have corrupted themselves: 8They have turned aside quickly out of the way which I commanded them: they have made them a molten calf, and have worshipped it, and have sacrificed thereunto, and said, These be thy gods, O Israel, which have brought thee up out of the land of Egypt. 9And the LORD said unto Moses, I have seen this people, and, behold, it is a stiff-necked people: 10Now therefore let me alone, that my wrath may wax hot against them, and that I may consume them: and I will make of thee a great nation. 11And Moses besought the LORD his God, and said, LORD, why doth thy wrath wax hot against thy people, which thou hast brought forth out of the land of Egypt with great power, and with a mighty hand? 12Wherefore should the Egyptians speak, and say, for mischief did he bring them out, to slay them in the mountains, and to consume them from the face of the earth? Turn from thy fierce wrath, and repent of this evil against thy people. 13Remember Abraham, Isaac, and Israel, thy servants, to whom thou sparest by thine own self, and sadist unto them, I will multiply your seed as the stars of heaven, and all this land that I have spoken of will I give unto your seed, and they shall inherit it forever. 14And the LORD repented of the evil which he thought to do unto his people. 15And Moses turned, and went down from the mount, and the two tables of the testimony were in his hand: the tables were written on both their sides; on the one side and on the other were they written. 16And the tables were the work of God, and the writing was the writing of God, graven upon the tables. 17And when Joshua heard the noise of the people as they shouted, he said unto Moses, There is a noise of war in the camp. 18And he said, it is not the voice of them that shout for mastery, neither is it the voice of them that cry for being overcome: but the noise of them that sing do I hear. 19And it came to pass, as soon as he came nigh unto the camp, that he saw the calf, and the dancing: and Moses' anger waxed hot, and he cast the tables out of his hands, and break them beneath the mount. 20And he took the calf which they had made, and burnt it in the fire, and ground it to powder, and strewed it upon the water, and made the children of Israel drink of it. 21And Moses said unto Aaron, What did this people unto thee, that thou hast brought so great a sin upon them? 22And Aaron said, Let not the anger of my lord wax hot: thou knows the people that they are Set on mischief. 23For they said unto me, Make us gods, which shall go before us: for as for this Moses, the man that brought us up out of the land of Egypt, we woot not what is become of him. 24And I said unto them, whosoever hath any gold, let them break it off.

So they gave it me: then I cast it into the fire, and there came out this calf. This is the problem today; people can't wait because they don't have patience. They are always getting into trouble because of someone else. If you listen to others, you will get into trouble with God and man. Moses stood in the gap for the people of Israel. Just like God's people are today, people will still sin behind your back. You have to keep an eye on them. God want somebody to live right behind closed doors. You don't have to see how you are coming out, just stay in line with the word of God, and you will come out on time. You can't rush God; he will be there on time. (Exodus 32:26) said, and when Moses saw that the people were naked; (for Aaron had made them naked unto their shame among their enemies :) 26Then Moses stood in the gate of the camp, and said, who is on the LORD'S side? let him come unto me. And all the sons of Levi gathered themselves together unto him. The ones that are on God's side need to come forth and pray. Together we can stand, but divided we will fall. Together we can win any fight on the Lord's side. (Matthew 12:50) says, 5And Jesus knew their thoughts, and said unto them, Every kingdom divided against itself is brought to desolation; and every city or house divided against itself shall not stand: 26And if Satan cast out Satan, he is divided against himself; how shall then his kingdom stand? 27And if I by Beelzebub cast out devils, by whom do your children cast them out? Therefore they shall be your judges. 28But if I cast out devils by the Spirit of God, then the kingdom of God is come unto you. 29Or else how can one enter into a strong man's house, and spoil his goods, except he first bind the strong man? And then he will spoil his house. 30He that is not with me is against me; and he that gathered not with me scattered abroad. 31Wherefore I say unto you, all manner of sin and blasphemy shall be forgiven unto men: but the blasphemy against the Holy Ghost shall not be forgiven unto men. 32And whosoever speaks a word against the Son of man, it shall be forgiven him: but whosoever speaks against the Holy Ghost, it shall not be forgiven him, neither in this world, and neither in the world to come. 33Either make the tree good, and his fruit good; or else make the tree corrupt, and his fruit corrupt: for the tree is known by his fruit. 34O generation of vipers, how can ye, being evil, speak good things? For out of the abundance of the heart the mouth speaks. 35A good man out of the good treasure of the heart brunet forth good things: and an evil man out of the evil treasure brunet forth evil things. 36But I say unto you, that every idle word that men shall speak, they shall give account thereof in the Day of Judgment. 37For by thy words thou shalt be justified, and by thy words thou shalt be condemned. 38Then certain of the scribes and of the Pharisees answered, saying, Master, we would see a sign from thee. 39But he answered and said unto them, An evil and adulterous generation seventh after a sign; and there shall no sign be given to it, but the sign of the prophet Jonas: 40For as Jonas was three days and three nights in the whale's belly; so shall the Son of man be three days and three nights in the heart of the earth. 41The men of Nineveh shall rise in judgment with this generation, and shall condemn it:

because they repented at the preaching of Jonas; and, behold, a greater than Jonas is here. 42The queen of the south shall rise up in the judgment with this generation, and shall condemn it: for she came from the uttermost parts of the earth to hear the Wisdom of Solomon; and, behold, a greater than Solomon is here.43 When the unclean spirit is gone out of a man, he walked through dry places, seeking rest, and fended none. 44Then he smith, I will return into my house from whence I came out; and when he is come, he fended it empty, swept, and garnished. 45Then Goethe he, and takes with himself seven other spirits more wicked than himself, and they enter in and dwell there: and the last state of that man is worse than the first. Even so shall it be also unto this wicked generation. 46While he yet talked to the people, behold, his mother and his brethren stood without, desiring to speak with him. 43 When the unclean spirit is gone out of a man, he walked through dry places, seeking rest, and fended none. 44Then he smith, I will return into my house from whence I came out; and when he is come, he fended it empty, swept, and garnished. 45Then Goethe he, and takes with himself seven other spirits more wicked than himself, and they enter in and dwell there: and the last state of that man is worse than the first.

Even so shall it be also unto this wicked generation. 46While he yet talked to the people, behold, his mother and his brethren stood without, desiring to speak with him. 47Then one said unto him, Behold, thy mother and thy brethren stand without, desiring to speak with thee. 48But he answered and said unto him that told him, who is my mother? And who are my brethren?

49And he stretched forth his hand toward his disciples, and said, Behold my mother and my brethren! 50For whosoever shall do the will of my Father which is in heaven, the same is my brother, and sister, and mother. Behold, thy mother and thy brethren stand without, desiring to speak with thee. 48But he answered and said unto him that told him, who is my mother? And who are my brethren? 49And he stretched forth his hand toward his disciples, and said, Behold my mother and my brethren! 50For whosoever shall do the will of my Father which is in heaven, the same is my brother, and sister, and mother. Now if you want to see the sign this is it. Whatever you are doing for God, don't stop. It makes no difference that comes, don't stop. Jesus doesn't come all the time when you call right then, but he is never late. Just pray and wait, Jesus was speaking to his disciples, and didn't stop. This lets us know God doesn't have a respectable person. What he will do for one, he will do for others. When Jesus went to the grave to raise the dead man, Lazarus, Mary and Martha thought he should come early, but Jesus knew what he could do. All he had to do was just call Lazarus out of the grave. Lazarus came forth and it didn't make a difference how long he had been there. It doesn't matter how long you have been dead in sin, one call to Jesus and you can come out of sin and live in Jesus. This lets us know it can and will be too late, so do it now while you have the chance.(Matthew 24:13) says, Let him which is on the housetop not come down to take any thing out of his house; (Matthew 24: 30-37) says, 0And then shall appear the sign of the Son of man in heaven: and then shall all the tribes of the earth mourn, and they shall see the Son of man coming in the clouds of heaven with power and great glory. 31And he shall send his angels with a great sound of a trumpet, and they shall gather together his elect from the four winds, from one end of heaven to the other. 32Now learn a parable of the fig tree; When his branch is yet tender, and putted forth leaves, ye know that summer is nigh: 33So likewise ye, when ye shall see all these things, know that it is near, even at the doors. 34Verily I say unto you, this generation shall not pass, till all these things are fulfilled. 35Heaven and earth shall pass away, but my words shall not pass away. 36But of that day and hour knows no man, no, not the angels of heaven, but my Father only.

But as the days of one were, so shall also the coming of the Son of man be. You can stop listening to man telling you when the world is going to end, because man doesn't know, only the father, which is in heaven. When your last breathe leave out of your body that is the end of your world; which ever way you leave, you don't have another chance. It will be the same thing over, just worse. (Matthew 24: 42) says, Watch therefore: for ye know not what hour your Lord doth come. We watch to warn. (Jeremiah 39:1-5) says, Woe is unto the pastors that destroy and scatter the sheep of my pasture! Smith the LORD. 2Therefore thus smith the LORD God of Israel against the pastors that feed my people; ye have scattered my flock, and driven them away, and have not visited them: behold, I will visit upon you the evil of your doings, smith the LORD. 3And I will gather the remnant of my flock out of all countries whither I have driven them, and will bring them again to their folds; and they shall be fruitful and increase. 4And I will set up shepherds over them which shall feed them: and they shall fear no more, nor be dismayed, neither shall they be lacking, smith the LORD. 5Behold, the days come, smith the LORD, that I will raise unto David a righteous Branch, and a King shall reign and prosper, and shall execute judgment and justice in the earth. Some people will be raised up that will obey God, and lose God's people. Everybody will not be harden and stiff-necked. Somebody will want the word of God. He said, preach whether they hear or whether they forebear. (Jeremiah 5:1-10) says, Run ye to and fro through the streets of Jerusalem, and see now, and know, and seek in the broad places thereof, if ye can find a man, if there be any that executed judgment, that seventh the truth; and I will pardon it. 2And though they say, The LORD lived; surely they swear falsely. 3O LORD, are not thine eyes upon the truth? Thou hast stricken them, but they have not grieved; thou hast consumed them, but they have refused to receive correction: they have made their faces harder than a rock; they have refused to return. 4Therefore I said, surely these are poor; they are foolish: for they know not the way of the LORD, nor the judgment of their God. 5I will get me unto the great men, and will speak unto them; for they have known the way of the LORD, and the judgment of their God: but these have altogether broken the yoke, and burst the bonds. 6Wherefore a lion out of the forest shall slay them, and a wolf of the evenings shall spoil them, a leopard shall watch over their cities: every one that Goethe out thence shall be torn in pieces:

because their transgressions are many, and their backslidings are increased. 7How shall I pardon thee for this? Thy children have forsaken me, and sworn by them that are no gods: when I had fed them to the full, they then committed adultery, and assembled themselves by troops in the harlots' houses. 8They were as fed horses in the morning: every one neighed after his neighbor's wife. 9Shall I not visit for these things? Smith the LORD: and shall not my soul be avenged on such a nation as this? 10Go ye up upon her walls, and destroy; but make not a full end: take away her battlements; for they are not the Lord's. (Jeremiah 6:17-19) says, 7Also I set watchmen over you, saying, Hearken to the sound of the trumpet.

But they said, we will not hearken. 18Therefore hear, ye nations, and know, O congregation, what is among them. 19Hear, O earth: behold, I will bring evil upon this people, even the fruit of their thoughts, because they have not hearkened unto my words, nor to my law, but rejected it. When you see things like this, they are a reminder that we have rejected the word of God, and God has also rejected us. He will make your ears heavy and your eyes dim, because you want to hear, (Isaiah 29:3-4) says, And I will camp against thee round about, and will lay siege against thee with a mount, and I will raise forts against thee. 4And thou shalt be brought down, and shalt speak out of the ground, and thy speech shall be low out of the dust, and thy voice shall be, as of one that hath a familiar spirit, out of the ground, and thy speech shall whisper out of the dust.(Isaiah 5:14-17) says, 4Therefore hell hath enlarged herself, and opened her mouth without measure: and their glory, and their multitude, and their pomp, and he that rejoiced, shall descend into it. 15And the mean man shall be brought down, and the mighty man shall be humbled, and the eyes of the lofty shall be humbled: 16But the LORD of hosts shall be exalted in judgment, and God that is holy shall be sanctified in righteousness. So this is why we warn you, don't let hell be your home. Once, there, you are never getting out. It is a one way journey. When we warn you, we take the blood off of our hands. This is the preached word. Those of you that have ears to hear, let them hear what the spirit is saying to the church. If we warn you and you don't take heed to the warning, the blood is on your hands and our hands are clean, but if we don't blow the trumpet, your blood will be on our hands, because God told us to do so. This is what you calling saving yourself from this evil generation. Do your job, no one can do it for you; not and you get paid and only what you do for Christ will last. Jesus said in (Matthew 24: 46-51), 6Blessed is that servant, whom his lord when he cometh shall find so doing. 47Verily I say unto you, that he shall make him ruler over all his goods. 48But and if that evil servant shall say in his heart, My lord delayed his coming; 49And shall begin to smite his fellow servants, and to eat and drink with the drunken; 50The lord of that servant shall come in a day when he looked not for him, and in an hour that he is not aware of, 51And shall cut him asunder, and appoint him his portion with the hypocrites: there shall be weeping and gnashing of teeth. We are talking about the spiritual work of God now. Continue in the word of God, be in the word when Jesus come back, if not you work will be in vain. In (Acts 2:1-) says, And when the day of Pentecost was fully come, they were all with one accord in one place. 2And suddenly there came a sound from heaven as of a rushing mighty wind, and it filled all the house where they were sitting. 3And there appeared unto them cloven tongues like as of fire, and it sat upon each of them. 4And they were all filled with the Holy Ghost, and began to speak with other tongues, as the Spirit gave them utterance. 5And there were dwelling at Jerusalem Jews, devout men, out of every nation under heaven. 6Now when this was noised abroad, the multitude came together, and was confounded, because that every man heard them speak in his own language. 7And they were all amazed and marveled, saying one to another, Behold, are not all these which speak Galileans? 8And how hear we every man in our own tongue, wherein we were born? God can do the things which seem impossible. The things he is able to do, man can't understand, but God had stepped in their hearts and their mind and brought about a change.

God sent like as a fire to burn up everything that were not like him, and he sent the wind to blow it away. He didn't just burn it, he blew it away as well. (Acts 2: 12-16) says, 2And they were all amazed, and were in doubt, saying one to another, What meant this? 13 Others mocking said, These men are full of new wine.14But Peter, standing up with the eleven, lifted up his voice, and said unto them, Ye men of Judaea, and all ye that dwell at Jerusalem, be this known unto you, and hearken to my words: 15For these are not drunken, as ye suppose, seeing it is but the third hour of the day. 16But this is that which was spoken by the prophet Joel. Somebody wanted to accuse them of being drunk with wine, but Peter stood up and said, these men are not drunk as you suppose, but he didn't say that they weren't drunk, but not as you suppose; it is but the third hour, the Liquor Store is not opened yet. What he was saying is they are not drunk in the Holy Ghost. What we need now is to get drunk on the new wine. Because what you are drinking now is the old, and it is making you sick. You need to get some new wine; I am talking about the Holy Ghost. Somebody said, "I been on cloud nine, when you try this wine, you can be twice as high; which will make you be on cloud eighteen. It doesn't leave you with a hangover; you can have it everyday, and be on a high like the Georgia pine. You can go higher if you just stay in line with the word. These people continued in the word. (Acts 2:40-47) says, 40And with many other words did he testify and exhort, saying, Save yourselves from this untoward generation. 41Then they that gladly received his word were baptized: and the same day there were added unto them about three thousand souls. 42And they continued steadfastly in the apostles' doctrine and fellowship, and in breaking of bread, and in prayers. 43And fear came upon every soul: and many wonders and signs were done by the apostles. 44And all that believed were together, and had all things common; 45And sold their possessions and goods, and parted them to all men, as every man had need. 46And they, continuing daily with one accord in the temple, and breaking bread from house to house, did eat their meat with gladness and singleness of heart, 47Praising

God, and having favor with all the people. And the Lord added to the church daily such as should be saved. You see, you can't stop, this is what I am now breaking bread to everyone that will eat. When the table is spread, if you don't eat, you will still starve to death. Anything you don't feed, will die. You can't eat one meal a week, and stay strong; you can't eat the word of God every now and then and stay strong, you can't just be strong; you have to get strong and stay strong. This is the same Holy Ghost that Peter, and John had when they went up to the Temple where this lame man was. (Acts 3:1-12) says, Now Peter and John went up together into the temple at the hour of prayer, being the ninth hour. 2And a certain man lame from his mother's womb was carried, whom they laid daily at the gate of the temple which is called Beautiful, to ask alms of them that entered into the temple; 3Who seeing Peter and John about to go into the temple asked an alms. 4And Peter, fastening his eyes upon him with John, said, Look on us. 5And he gave heed unto them, expecting to receive something of them. 6Then Peter said, Silver and gold have I none; but such as I have give I thee: In the name of Jesus Christ of Nazareth rise up and walk. 7And he took him by the right hand, and lifted him up: and immediately his feet and ankle bones received strength. 8And he leaping up stood, and walked, and entered with them into the temple, walking, and leaping, and praising God. 9And all the people saw him walking and praising God: 10And they knew that it was he which sat for alms at the Beautiful gate of the temple: and they were filled with wonder and amazement at that which had happened unto him. 11And as the lame man which was healed held Peter and John, all the people ran together unto them in the porch that is called Solomon's, greatly wondering. 12And when Peter saw it, he answered unto the people, ye men of Israel, why marvel ye at this? Or why look ye so earnestly on us, as though by our own power or holiness we had made this man to walk? O, praise God, glorify him. Peter was letting the people know that he and John didn't do that, but the power of God through them.

When someone is healed through you, you don't get the glory, the glory belongs to God. God worked through a man and a woman. So choose this day that you are going to serve. (Joshua 24:14-20) says, 14Now therefore fear the LORD, and serve him in sincerity and in truth: and put away the gods which your fathers served on the other side of the flood, and in Egypt; and serve ye the LORD. 15And if it seem evil unto you to serve the LORD, choose you this day whom ye will serve; whether the gods which your fathers served that were on the other side of the flood, or the gods of the Amorites, in whose land ye dwell: but as for me and my house, we will serve the LORD. 16And the people answered and said, God forbid that we should forsake the LORD, to serve other gods; 17For the LORD our God, he it is that brought us up and our fathers out of the land of Egypt, from the house of bondage, and which did those great signs in our sight, and preserved us in all the way wherein we went, and among all the people through whom we passed: 18And the LORD drive out from before us all the people, even the Amorites which dwelt in the land: therefore will we also serve the LORD; for he is our God. 19And Joshua said unto the people, ye cannot serve the LORD: for he is an holy God; he is a jealous God; he will not forgive your transgressions nor your sins. 20If ye forsake the LORD, and serve strange gods, then he will turn and do you hurt, and consume you, after that he hath done you good. So we see in the will of God, we can be blessed and we can make a change and if we turn from God, he will turn from us, and we will be cursed by the same God; because God is a jealous God. If you are going to serve God, then serve God, if you are going to serve Ba-al, look at what you are you doing to yourself. Whether it is for God or Baal, you will have to give in to account for your decision. The one you choose is the one that will pay you and you will have a payday. Whatever you do, just does it well, because it is either heaven or hell. (Isaiah 5:14-30) says, 14Therefore hell hath enlarged herself, and opened her mouth without measure: and their glory, and their multitude, and their pomp, and he that rejoiced, shall descend into it. 15And the mean man shall be brought down, and the mighty man shall be humbled, and the eyes of the lofty shall be humbled: 16But the LORD of hosts shall be exalted in judgment, and God that is holy shall be sanctified in righteousness. 17Then shall the lambs feed after their manner, and the waste places of the fat ones shall strangers eat. 18Woe unto them that draw iniquity with cords of vanity, and sin as it were with a cart rope: 19That say, Let him make speed, and hasten his work, that we may see it: and let the counsel of the Holy One of Israel draw nigh and come, that we may know it! 20Woe unto them that call evil good, and good evil; that put darkness for light, and light for darkness; that put bitter for sweet, and sweet for bitter! 21Woe unto them that is wise in their own eyes, and prudent in their own sight! 22Woe unto them that are mighty to drink wine, and men of strength to mingle strong drink: 23Which justify the wicked for reward, and take away the righteousness of the righteous from him! 24Therefore as the fire devoured the stubble, and the flame consumed the chaff, so their root shall be as rottenness, and their blossom shall go up as dust: because they have cast away the law of the LORD of hosts, and despised the word of the Holy One of Israel. 25Therefore is the anger of the LORD kindled against his people, and he hath stretched forth his hand against them, and hath smitten them: and the hills did tremble, and their carcasseswere torn in the midst of the streets. For all this his anger is not turned away, but his hand is stretched out still. 26And he will lift up an ensign to the nations from far, and will hiss unto them from the end of the earth: and, behold, they shall come with speed swiftly: 27None shall be weary nor stumble among them; none shall slumber nor sleep; neither shall the girdle of their loins be loosed, nor the latchet of their shoes be broken: 28Whose arrows are sharp, and all their bows bent, their horses' hoofs shall be counted like flint, and their wheels like a whirlwind: 29Their roaring shall be like a lion, they shall roar like young lions: yea, they shall roar, and lay hold of the prey, and shall carry it away safe, and none shall deliver it. 30And in that day they shall roar against them like the roaring of the sea: and if one look unto the land, behold darkness and sorrow, and the light is darkened in the heavens thereof.

We know that destruction is in the land, but God is still standing with an outstretched hand, still giving us a choice. (1Thessalonians 5:1-18) says, but of the times and the seasons, brethren, ye have no need that I write unto you. 2For yourselves know perfectly that the day of the Lord so cometh as a thief in the night. 3For when they shall say, Peace and safety; then sudden destruction cometh upon them, as travail upon a woman with child; and they shall not escape. 4But ye, brethren, are not in darkness, that that day should overtake you as a thief. 5Ye are all the children of light, and the children of the day: we are not of the night, nor of darkness. 6Therefore let us not sleep, as do others; but let us watch and be sober. 7For they that sleep in the night; and they that are drunken are drunken in the night. 8But let us, who are of the day, be sober, putting on the breastplate of faith and love; and for an helmet, the hope of salvation. 9For God hath not appointed us to wrath, but to obtain salvation by our Lord Jesus Christ, 10Who died for us, that, whether we wake or sleep, we should live together with him. Wherefore comfort yourselves together, and edify one another, even as also ye do. 12And we beseech you, brethren, to know them which labor among you, and are over you in the Lord, and admonish you; 13And to esteem them very highly in love for their work's sake. And be at peace among yourselves. 14Now we exhort you, brethren, warn them that are unruly, comfort the feebleminded, support the weak, and be patient toward all men. 15See that none render evil for evil unto any man; but ever follow that which is good, both among yourselves, and to all men. 16Rejoice evermore. 17Pray without ceasing. 18In every thing gives thanks: for this is the will of God in Christ Jesus concerning you. The word is saying to us, in this day and hour, we are to know those that labor among us, know the one that is preaching and teaching. We are suppose to know the truth if we are the people of light, edify one another, encourage your sister and brother, and always be sober, and give respect to all men, and give thanks for everything God do for you. Be thankful over a few things and God will make you ruler over many. (Matthew 25: 21-23) says, 1 His lord said unto him, well done, thou good and faithful servant: thou hast been faithful over a few things, I will make thee ruler over many things: enter thou into the joy of thy lord. 22 He also that had received two talents came and said, Lord, thou deliverers unto me two talents: behold, I have gained two other talents beside them. 23His lord said unto him, well done, good and faithful servant; thou hast been faithful over a few things, I will make thee ruler over many things: enter thou into the joy of thy lord. God will not bless a greedy person because they always want more. Just be thankful for what God has done. When he blesses you with anything, and yon don't use it right, or use it for the uplifting of the house of God, he will take it from you and give it to someone else. If yon can sing, and don't use your voice, God will give it to someone else.

Whatever we have, we are to use it, and that means everything; if not he will take it all back. (Matthew 10:8-) says, heal the sick, cleanse the lepers, and raise the dead, cast out devils: freely ye have received, freely give. The word talking about receiving and giving. It means when you learn about Jesus, tell somebody about him, which is the best gift. When you know the truth tells somebody about it. What is the truth? (John 14:6-7) says, Jesus smith unto him, I am the way, the truth, and the life: no man cometh unto the Father, but by me. 7If ye had known me, ye should have known my Father also: and from henceforth ye know him, and have seen him. Once you receive the truth, what are you still looking for? (Galatians 1:6-12) says, I marvel that ye are so soon removed from him that called you into the grace of Christ unto another gospel: 7Which is not another; but there be some that trouble you, and would pervert the gospel of Christ. 8But though we, or an angel from heaven, preach any other gospel unto you than that which we have preached unto you, let him be accursed. 9As we said before, so say I now again, if any man preaches any other gospel unto you than that ye have received, let him be accursed. 10For do I now persuade men, or God? Or do I seek to please men? For if I yet pleased men, I should not be the servant of Christ. 11But I certify you, brethren that the gospel which was preached of me is not after man. 12For I neither received it of man, neither was I taught it, but by the revelation of Jesus Christ. You can't please man, just obey God. When a man pleases the flesh, the spirit and the flesh war against one another. (James 4:4-6) says, 1From whence come wars and fighting's among you? Come they not hence, even of your lusts that war in your members? 2Ye lust, and have not: ye kill, and desire to have, and cannot obtain:

ye fight and war, yet ye have not, because ye ask not. 3Ye ask, and receive not, because ye ask amiss, that ye may consume it upon your lusts. 4Ye adulterers and adulteresses know ye not that the friendship of the world is enmity with God? Whosoever therefore will be a friend of the world is the enemy of God. 5 Do ye think that the scripture smith in vain, the spirit that dwelled in us lusted to envy? 6But he giveth more grace. Wherefore he smith, God resisted the proud, but giveth grace unto the humble. Jesus loves a humble spirit. (James 4: 7-17) says, 7Submit yourselves therefore to God. Resist the devil, and he will flee from you. 8Draw nigh to God, and he will draw nigh to you. Cleanse your hands, ye sinners; and purify your hearts, ye double minded. 9Be afflicted, and mourn, and weep: let your laughter be turned to mourning, and your joy to heaviness. 10Humble yourselves in the sight of the Lord, and he shall lift you up.11Speak not evil one of another, brethren.

He that speaks evil of his brother, and judged his brother, speaks evil of the law, and judged the law: but if thou judge the law, thou art not a doer of the law, but a judge. 12There is one lawgiver, who is able to save and to destroy: who art thou that judge another? 13Go to now, ye that say, to day or to morrow we will go into such a city, and continue there a year, and buy and sell, and get gain: 14Whereas ye know not what shall be on the morrow. For what is your life? It is even a vapor that appeared for a little time, and then vanished away. 15For that ye ought to say, if the Lord will, we shall live, and do this, or that. 16But now ye rejoice in your boastings: all such rejoicing is evil.

17Therefore to him that knows to do good, and doeth it not, to him it is sin. The word is letting us know it is better not to know the word, than to know it and don't so anything about it. When you sit under the word and hear it, you are taking in damnation to your soul. Someone might say, I go to church every Sunday. That is what I am talking about; taking in damnation to your soul. Your work is an outside work, which will show you up one day. When it is time to meet Jesus. (Revelation 2:2-7) says, I know thy works, and thy labor, and thy patience, and how thou canst not bear them which are evil: and thou hast tried them which say they are apostles, and are not, and hast found them liars: 3And hast borne, and hast patience, and for my name's sake hast labored, and hast not fainted. 4Nevertheless I have somewhat against thee, because thou hast left thy first love. 5Remember therefore from whence thou art fallen, and repent, and do the first works; or else I will come unto thee quickly, and will remove thy candlestick out of his place, except thou repent. 6But this thou hast, that thou hates the deeds of the Nicolai tans, which I also hate. 7He that hath an ear, let him hear what the Spirit smith unto the churches; to him that overcomes will I give to eat of the tree of life, which is in the midst of the paradise of God. 1We need to know we can't live this life alone. Together we stand, divided we fall. It will come a time that you will need someone to talk to. (Proverbs 18: 24) says, 24A man that hath friends must shew himself friendly: and there is a friend that ticket closer than a brother. 2 You have to trust somebody. (Ecclesiastes 4:8-12) says, 8There is one alone, and there is not a second; yea, he hath neither child nor brother: yet is there no end of all his labor; neither is his eye satisfied with riches; neither smith he, for whom does I labor, and bereave my soul of good? This is also vanity, yea, it is a sore travail. 9Two are better than one; because they have a good reward for their labor. 10For if they fall, the one will lift up his fellow: but woe to him that is alone when he fillet; for he hath not another to help him up. 11Again, if two lie together, then they have heat: but how can one be warm alone? 12And if one prevail against him, two shall withstand him; and a threefold cord is not quickly broken. 3 Together we have strength and are not so easy to be brought down. (Isaiah 40: 29-) says, 9He giveth power to the faint; and to them that have no might he increased strength. 30Even the youths shall faint and be weary and the young men shall utterly fall: 31But they that wait upon the LORD shall renew their strength; they shall mount up with wings as eagles; they shall run, and not be weary; and they shall walk, and not faint. 4Jesus sent his disciples out two by two. (Amos 3:3-8) says, Can two walk together, except they are agreed? 4Will a lion roar in the forest, when he hath no prey? Will a young lion cry out of his den, if he has taken nothing? 5Can a bird falls in a snare upon the earth, where no gin is for him? Shall one take up a snare from the earth, and have taken nothing at all? 6Shall a trumpet is blown in the city, and the people not be afraid? Shall there be evil in a city, and the LORD hath not done it? 7Surely the Lord GOD will do nothing, but he revealed his secret unto his servants the prophets. 8The lion hath roared, who will not fear? The Lord GOD hath spoken, who can but prophesy? 5 (Acts 4:20-) says, 20For we cannot but speak the things which we have seen and heard6 I don't have a lie to tell you.

I speak when the spirit speaks; my words will not help. What I know I count. I count it as dong. I can help you and you can help me. We are the people that God is looking for to come forth. We might not always agree. (Isaiah 1: 18-20) says, 8Come now, and let us reason together, smith the LORD: though your sins be as scarlet, they shall be as white as snow; though they be red like crimson, they shall be as wool. 19If ye be willing and obedient, ye shall eat the good of the land: 20But if ye refuse and rebel, ye shall be devoured with the sword: for the mouth of the LORD hath spoken it. 7 We know all we have to do is be willing and obedient to God to receive his blessings. If God said it, it is true because God don't go back on his word. When we get together we will see god move. You might not see eye to eye, sit down and talk bout it. How do you expect one to understand when he doesn't know what is wrong? Sit down, talk about it, and straighten it out. Whatever the problem is God will straighten it out if you let him. I hear some people saying my people in my church, they are God's people. And God said, if my people which are called by my name shall humble themselves, and pray and seek my face, and turn from their wicked ways, then I will hear from heaven and will forgive their sin and heal their land. So we see here the people belong to God. You are just their servant and then he said, Up on this rock I will build my church and the gates of hell shall not prevail against it (Matthew 16: 18). We see here that the church belong to God and he left the preachers in charge. (Matthew 16: 19) says, and I will give unto thee the keys of the kingdom of heaven: and whatsoever thou shalt bind on earth shall be bound in heaven: and whatsoever thou shalt loose on earth shall be loosed in heaven. 8 You see, God's preacher do have charge to keep and a God to glorify. (2:Corinthians 4:1) says, 1Therefore seeing we have this ministry, as we have received mercy, we faint not; 2But have renounced the hidden things of dishonesty, not walking in craftiness, nor handling the word of God deceitfully; but by manifestation of the truth commending ourselves to every man's conscience in the sight of God. 3But if our gospel be hid, it is hid to them that are lost: 4In whom the god of this world hath blinded the minds of them which believe not, lest the light of the glorious gospel of Christ, who is the image of God, should shine unto them. 5For we preach not ourselves, but Christ Jesus the Lord; and ourselves your servants for Jesus' sake. 6For God, who commanded the light to shine out of darkness, hath shined in our hearts, to give the light of the knowledge of the glory of God in the face of Jesus Christ. 7But we have this treasure in earthen vessels that the Excellency of the power may be of God, and not of us. 8We are troubled on every side, yet not distressed; we are perplexed, but not in despair; 9Persecuted, but not forsaken; cast down, but not destroyed; 10Always bearing about in the body the dying of the Lord Jesus, that the life also of Jesus might be made manifest in our body. 11For we which live are always delivered unto death for Jesus' sake, that the life also of Jesus might be made manifest in our mortal flesh. 12So then death worked in us, but life in you. 13 We having the same spirit of faith, according as it is written, I believed, and therefore have I spoken; we also believe, and therefore speak; 14Knowing that he which raised up the Lord Jesus shall raise up us also by Jesus, and shall present us with you. 15For all things are for your sakes, that the abundant grace might through the thanksgiving of many redound to the glory of God. 16For which cause we faint not; but though our outward man perishes, yet the inward man is renewed day by day. 17For our light affliction, which is but for a moment, worked for us a far more exceeding and eternal weight of glory; 18While we look not at the things which are seen, but at the things which are not seen: for the things which are seen are temporal; but the things which are not seen are eternal.

So we see what we are looking at now. It is not going to help us later, so wait on that which are not seen, don't always chose the green side, and wait on it to turn brown. Chose the brown side and wait on it to turn green. Waiting is better because you know it is getting green someday. (2:Corinthians 5:1-15) says, 1For we know that if our earthly house of this tabernacle were dissolved, we have a building of God, an house not made with hands, eternal in the heavens. 2For in this we groan, earnestly desiring to be clothed upon with our house which is from heaven: 3If so be that being clothed we shall not be found naked. 4For we that are in this tabernacle do groan, being burdened: not for that we would be unclothed, but clothed upon, that mortality might be swallowed up of life. 5Now he that hath wrought us for the selfsame thing is God, who also hath given unto us the earnest of the Spirit. 6Therefore we are always confident, knowing that, whilst we are at home in the body, we are absent from the Lord: 7(For we walk by faith, not by sight:) 8We are confident, I say, and willing rather to be absent from the body, and to be present with the Lord. 9Wherefore we labor, that, whether present or absent, we may be accepted of him. 10For we must all appear before the judgment seat of Christ; that every one may receive the things done in his body, according to that he hath done, whether it is good or bad. 11Knowing therefore the terror of the Lord, we persuade men; but we are made manifest unto God; and I trust also are made manifest in your consciences. 12For we commend not ourselves again unto you, but give you occasion to glory on our behalf, that ye may have somewhat to answer them which glory in appearance, and not in heart. 13For whether we are beside ourselves, it is to God: or whether we are sober, it is for your cause. 14For the love of Christ constrained us; because we thus judge, that if one died for all, then were all dead: 15And that he died for all, that they which live should not henceforth live unto themselves, but unto him which died for them, and rose again. 9We know Jesus died for all of us, but he didn't stay dead. If you are dead, get up; you don't have to stay dead either. Rise up in Jesus. (1: Corinthians 15: 55-57) says, O death, where is thy sting? O grave, where is thy victory? 56 The sting of death is sin; and the strength of sin is the law. 510Thank God because he gives us the victory through our Lord, Jesus Christ. Therefore, my beloved brethren be ye steadfast, unmovable always abounding in the work of the Lord. Forasmuch as ye know that your labor is not in vain in the Lord. Stand still and see the salvation of the Lord unmovable. (Luke 13:24-30) says, 24Strive to enter in at the strait gate: for many, I say unto you, will seek to enter in, and shall not be able. 25When once the master of the house is risen up, and hath shut to the door, and ye begin to stand without, and to knock at the door, saying, Lord, Lord, open unto us; and he shall answer and say unto you, I know you not whence ye are: 26Then shall ye begin to say, We have eaten and drunk in thy presence, and thou hast taught in our streets. 27But he shall say, I tell you, I know you not whence ye are; depart from me, all ye workers of iniquity. 28There shall be weeping and gnashing of teeth, when ye shall see Abraham, and Isaac, and Jacob, and all the prophets, in the kingdom of God, and you yourselves thrust out. 29And they shall come from the east, and from the west, and from the north, and from the south, and shall sit down in the kingdom of God. 30And, behold, there are last which shall be first, and there are first which shall be last.11We see here we don't have to worry about who get there first or who sits in the front seat. No one can save you a seat. You have to earn it for yourself. There want be no big eyes or little you. We will all be the same in the sight of God. You don't have to worry about who will be the greatest in heaven. When the question was asked to Jesus, (Matthew 18:1-7) says, at the same time came the disciples unto Jesus, saying, who is the greatest in the kingdom of heaven? 2And Jesus called a little child unto him, and set him in the midst of them, 3And said, Verily I say unto you, Except ye be converted, and become as little children, ye shall not enter into the kingdom of heaven. 4Whosoever therefore shall humble himself as this little child, the same is greatest in the kingdom of heaven. 5And whoso shall receive one such little child in my name received me. 6But whoso shall offend one of these little ones which believe in me, it were better for him that a millstone were hanged about his neck, and that he were drowned in the depth of the sea.7Woe unto the world because of offences! For it must needs be that offences come; but woe to that man by whom the offence cometh!12Now Jesus said these things would come, but he didn't say I had to partake in them.

This is why Jesus came so that he could take away the sins of the world. (Ephesians 1: 7-23) says, In whom we have redemption through his blood, the forgiveness of sins, according to the riches of his grace; 8Wherein he hath abounded toward us in all wisdom and prudence; 9Having made known unto us the mystery of his will, according to his good pleasure which he hath purposed in himself: 10That in the dispensation of the fullness of times he might gather together in one all things in Christ, both which are in heaven, and which are on earth; even in him: 11In whom also we have obtained an inheritance, being predestinated according to the purpose of him who worked all things after the counsel of his own will: 12That we should be to the praise of his glory, who first trusted in Christ. 13In whom ye also trusted, after that ye heard the word of truth, the gospel of your salvation: in whom also after that ye believed, ye were sealed with that holy Spirit of promise, 14Which is the earnest of our inheritance until the redemption of the purchased possession, unto the praise of his glory.

15Wherefore I also, after I heard of your faith in the Lord Jesus, and love unto all the saints, 16Cease not to give thanks for you, making mention of you in my prayers; 17That the God of our Lord Jesus Christ, the Father of glory, may give unto you the spirit of wisdom and revelation in the knowledge of him: 18The eyes of your understanding being enlightened; that ye may know what is the hope of his calling, and what the riches of the glory of his inheritance in the saints, 19And what is the exceeding greatness of his power to us-ward who believe, according to the working of his mighty power, 20Which he wrought in Christ, when he raised him from the dead, and set him at his own right hand in the heavenly places, 21Far above all principality, and power, and might, and dominion, and every name that is named, not only in this world, but also in that which is to come: 22And hath put all things under his feet, and gave him to be the head over all things to the church, 23Which is his body, the fullness of him that fillet all in all. 13Jesus came, he died, and rose; what more do you need to prove that he is alive forever more? Now you know the truth. (Matthew 24: 11-16) says, and many false prophets shall rise, and shall deceive many. 12And because iniquity shall abound, the love of many shall wax cold. 13But he that shall endure unto the end, the same shall be saved. 14And this gospel of the kingdom shall be preached in all the world for a witness unto all nations; and then shall the end come. 15When ye therefore shall see the abomination of desolation, spoken of by Daniel the prophet, stand in the holy place, (whoso breadth, let him understand).14 (Colossians 2: 9-14) says, for in him dwelled all the fullness of the Godhead bodily. 10And ye are complete in him, which is the head of all principality and power: 11In whom also ye are circumcised with the circumcision made without hands, in putting off the body of the sins of the flesh by the circumcision of Christ: 12Buried with him in baptism, wherein also ye are risen with him through the faith of the operation of God, who hath raised him from the dead.

13And you, being dead in your sins and the circumcision of your flesh, hath he quickened together with him, having forgiven you all trespasses; 14Blotting out the handwriting of ordinances that was against us, which was contrary to us, and took it out of the way, nailing it to his cross; 15 There will be many that will come and try to change the truth into a lie, but God is giving us time to get it right with him and believe the truth. There will come strong delusion trying to persuade you. (Matthew 24: 22-26) says, 22And except those days should be shortened, there should no flesh be saved: but for the elect's sake those days shall be shortened. 23Then if any man shall say unto you, Lo, here is Christ, or there; believe it not. 24For there shall arise false Christ's, and false prophets, and shall shew great signs and wonders; insomuch that, if it were possible, they shall deceive the very elect. 25Behold, I have told you before. 26Wherefore if they shall say unto you, Behold, he is in the desert; go not forth: behold, he is in the secret chambers; believe it not.16This is why God want his people to get up and get right and get real, because God's people are scattered. Let's get them back to the fold, and go out on the field and stay out there, calling all the preachers, and teachers. Find you job. (Matthew 9: 35-38) says, And Jesus went about all the cities and villages, teaching in their synagogues, and preaching the gospel of the kingdom, and healing every sickness and every disease among the people. 36But when he saw the multitudes, he was moved with compassion on them, because they fainted, and were scattered abroad, as sheep having no shepherd. 37Then smith he unto his disciples, the harvest truly is plenteous, but the laborers are few; 38Pray ye therefore the Lord of the harvest, that he will send forth laborers into his harvest. 17 We don't have to worry about having a job with Jesus. Just get in the word, Jesus said, Go into the vineyard and work, and whatever is right, I will pay. Don't worry about the next person, just do whatever comes to your hand, jus do what the Lord says to do. (Matthew 10: 16-) says, 6Behold, I send you forth as sheep in the midst of wolves: be ye therefore wise as serpents, and harmless as doves. 17But beware of men: for they will deliver you up to the councils, and they will scourge you in their synagogues; 18And ye shall be brought before governors and kings for my sake, for a testimony against them and the Gentiles. 19But when they deliver you up, take no thought how or what ye shall speak: for it shall be given you in that same hour what ye shall speak. 20For it is not ye that speak, but the Spirit of your Father which speaks in you.18 (John 12: 42-50) says, 2Nevertheless among the chief rulers also many believed on him; but because of the

Pharisees they did not confess him, lest they should be put out of the synagogue: 43For they loved the praise of men more than the praise of God. 44 Jesus cried and said, He that believeth on me, believeth not on me, but on him that sent me. 45And he that seethe me seethe him that sent me. 46I am come a light into the world, that whosoever believeth on me should not abide in darkness. 47And if any man hears my words, and believes not, I judge him not: for I came not to judge the world, but to save the world. 48He that rejected me, and received not my words, hath one that judged him: the word that I have spoken, the same shall judge him in the last day. 49For I have not spoken of myself; but the Father which sent me, he gave me a commandment, what I should say, and what I should speak. 50And I know that his commandment is life everlasting: whatsoever I speak therefore, even as the Father said unto me, so I speak. 19Jesus is offering a live eternal with him, but if we reject it that is our fault because we can't finds no fault in Jesus. Yes, we know we were born in sin.

This is why we must be born again. (John 3:1-21) says, There was a man of the Pharisees, named Nicodemus, a ruler of the Jews: 2The same came to Jesus by night, and said unto him, Rabbi, we know that thou art a teacher come from God: for no man can do these miracles that thou doest, except God be with him. 3Jesus answered and said unto him, Verily, verily, I say unto thee, except a man be born again, he cannot see the kingdom of God. 4Nicodemus smith unto him, how can a man be born when he is old? Can he enter the second time into his mother's womb, and be born?

5Jesus answered, Verily, verily, I say unto thee, except a man is born of water and of the Spirit, he cannot enter into the kingdom of God. 6That which is born of the flesh is flesh; and that which is born of the Spirit is spirit. 7Marvel not that I said unto thee, ye must be born again. 8The wind blotch where it listed, and thou headrest the sound thereof, but canst not tell whence it cometh, and whither it Goethe: so is every one that is born of the Spirit. 9Nicodemus answered and said unto him, how can these things be? 10Jesus answered and said unto him, Art thou a master of Israel, and knows not these things? 11Verily, verily, I say unto thee, we speak that we do know, and testify that we have seen; and ye receive not our witness. 12If I have told you earthly things, and ye believe not, how shall ye believe, if I tell you of heavenly things? 13And no man hath ascended up to heaven, but he that came down from heaven, even the Son of man which is in heaven. 14And as Moses lifted up the serpent in the wilderness, even so must the Son of man be lifted up: 15That whosoever believeth in him should not perish, but have eternal life. 16For God so loved the world that he gave his only begotten Son, that whosoever believeth in him should not perish, but have everlasting life. 17For God sent not his Son into the world to condemn the world; but that the world through him might be saved. 18He that believeth on him is not condemned: but he that believeth not is condemned already, because he hath not believed in the name of the only begotten Son of God. 19And this is the condemnation, that light is come into the world, and men loved darkness rather than light, because their deeds were evil. 20For every one that doeth evil hadith the light, neither cometh to the light, lest his deeds should be reproved. 21But he that doeth truth cometh to the light, that his deeds may be made manifest, that they are wrought in God. 20 There is no need to marvel at the word of God, if God said it, then it must be done. Jesus said we must be born again, to be born out of sin. God sent his only begotten son, his son was begotten by the Holy Ghost, a son with guile in his mouth. When he was on his way to the cross, he went down but he got up. He is letting us know if we fall down, we can get up. Don't stay down there and wallow, get up and try again. (Matthew 10: 22) says, 2And ye shall be hated of all men for my name's sake: but he that endured to the end shall be saved. 21 It will be a hear, so endure all hardship. Look to the hill which comes your help. (Psalm 121: 1-8) says, I will lift up mine eyes unto the hills, from whence cometh my help. 2My help cometh from the LORD, which made heaven and earth. 3He will not suffer thy foot to be moved: he that kept thee will not slumber. 4Behold, he that kept Israel shall neither slumber nor sleep. 5The LORD is thy keeper: the LORD is thy shade upon thy right hand. 6The sun shall not smite thee by day, nor the moon by night. 7The LORD shall preserve thee from all evil: he shall preserve thy soul. 8The LORD shall preserve thy going out and thy coming in from this time forth, and even for evermore. 22 (Hebrews 12: 1-13) says, Wherefore seeing we also are compassed about with so great a cloud of witnesses, let us lay aside every weight, and the sin which doth so easily beset us, and let us run with patience the race that is set before us, 2Looking unto Jesus the author and finisher of our faith; who for the joy that was set before him endured the cross, despising the shame, and is set down at the right hand of the throne of God. 3For consider him that endured such contradiction of sinners against himself, lest ye be wearied and faint in your minds. 4Ye have not yet resisted unto blood, striving against sin. 5And ye have forgotten the exhortation which speaks unto you as unto children, my son, despise not thou the chastening of the neither Lord, nor faint when thou art rebuked of him: 6For whom the Lord loved he chastened, and scourged every son whom he received. 7If ye endure chastening, God dealt with you as with sons; for what son is he whom the father chastened not? 8But if ye be without chastisement, whereof all are partakers, then are ye bastards, and not sons. 9Furthermore we have had fathers of our flesh which corrected us, and we gave them reverence: shall we not much rather be in subjection unto the Father of spirits, and live? 10For they verily for a few days chastened us after their own pleasure; but he for our profit, that we might be partakers of his holiness. 11Now no chastening for the present seemed to be joyous, but grievous: nevertheless afterward it yielded the peaceable fruit of righteousness unto them which are exercised thereby. 12Wherefore lift up the hands which hang down, and the feeble knees; 13And make straight paths for your feet, lest that which is lame be turned out of the way; but let it rather be healed. 23It is time to get concerned about your soul. (2 Peter 2: 4-6) says, 4For if God spared not the angels that sinned, but cast them down to hell, and delivered them into chains of darkness, to be reserved unto judgment; 5And spared not the old world, but saved Noah the eighth person, a preacher of righteousness, bringing in the flood upon the world of the ungodly; 6And turning the cities of Sodom and Gomorrah into ashes condemned them with an overthrow, making them an ensample unto those that after should live ungodly; 24Most people are not taking heed to the word of God, but listen, God is speaking, you need to hear God's word.

(Amos 4: 9-12) says, 9I have smitten you with blasting and mildew: when your gardens and your vineyards and your fig trees and your olive trees increased, the palmerworm devoured them: yet have ye not returned unto me, smith the LORD. 10I have sent among you the pestilence after the manner of Egypt: your young men have I slain with the sword and have taken away your horses; and I have made the stink of your camps to come up unto your nostrils: yet have ye not returned unto me, smith the LORD. 11I have overthrown some of you, as God overthrew Sodom and Gomorrah, and ye were as a firebrand plucked out of the burning: yet have ye not returned unto me, smith the LORD. 12Therefore thus will I do unto thee, O Israel: and because I will do this unto thee, prepare to meet thy God, O Israel.25God is saying out of this thing unto you, you still will not change. We see so much happening today; unlock your mind, if you can't see you know we are living in the end time. The word didn't say see the word said hear the word of God. Those of you that have ears to hear, let them hear what the spirit is saying to the church.(Mark 7: 37) says, and were beyond measure astonished, saying, He hath done all things well: he makes both the deaf to hear, and the dumb to speak. 26 God can use whoso ever he wants to. When you turn your back to him, what will it take for people to get back with God? We are being destroyed before our own faces, but yet we are turning a deaf ear to the word of God. Satan will use you until he uses you up and he doesn't have anything to pay you with but hell and destruction. (Philippians 3: 19-21) says, whose end is destruction, whose God is their belly, and whose glory is in their shame, who mind earthly things.) 20For our conversation is in heaven; from whence also we look for the Savior, the Lord Jesus Christ: 21Who shall change our vile body that it may be fashioned like unto his glorious body, according to the working whereby he is able even to subdue all things unto himself. 27 (Revelation 2: 7) says that hath an ear, let him hear what the Spirit smith unto the churches; to him that overcomes will I give to eat of the tree of life, which is in the midst of the paradise of God. 28 This is your reward from God. If you ankle down in the word of God, make sure your ankle holds. (Proverbs 18: 1-8) says, 1Through desire a man, having separated himself, seventh and intermeddled with all wisdom. 2A fool hath no delight in understanding, but that his heart may discover itself. 3When the wicked cometh, then cometh also contempt, and with ignominy reproach. 4The words of a man's mouth are as deep waters, and the wellspring of wisdom as a flowing brook. 5It is not good to accept the person of the wicked, to overthrow the righteous in judgment. 6A fool's lips enter into contention, and his mouth called for strokes. 7A fool's mouth is his destruction, and his lips are the snare of his soul. 8The words of a talebearer are as wounds, and they go down into the innermost parts of the belly29Don't try to take sin and stand against righteousness, because, when you do, you are bringing down yourself, because righteousness will stand. Your lips can only get you in trouble and cause you to be showed up as a fool. Sometimes you end up sick, just say I did this. A fool's mouth will cause his own destruction and his lips are the snare of his soul.

So be careful with your words, you can speak damnation on your own soul. (Psalms 14: 9) says, the fool hath said in his heart, There is no God. They are corrupt, they have done abominable works, there is none that doeth good.30(Proverbs 14: 9-12) says, Fools make a mock at sin: but among the righteous there is favor. 10The heart knows his own bitterness; and a stranger doth not intermeddle with his joy. 11The house of the wicked shall be overthrown: but the tabernacle of the upright shall flourish. 12There is a way which seemed right unto a man, but the end thereof is the ways of death.31(Proverbs 1: 7) says, he fear of the LORD is the beginning of knowledge: but fools despise wisdom and instruction. 32 (Proverbs 1: 24-30) says, Because I have called, and ye refused; I have stretched out my hand, and no man regarded; 25But ye have set at naught all my counsel, and would none of my reproof: 26I also will laugh at your calamity; I will mock when your fear cometh; 27When your fear cometh as desolation, and your destruction cometh as a whirlwind; when distress and anguish cometh upon you. 28Then shall they call upon me, but I will not answer; they shall seek me early, but they shall not find me: 29For that they hated knowledge, and did not choose the fear of the LORD: 30They would none of my counsel: they despised all my reproof. 31Therefore shall they eat of the fruit of their own way, and be filled with their own devices. 32For the turning away of the simple shall slay them, and the prosperity of fools shall destroy them. 33But whoso hearkened unto me shall dwell safely, and shall be quiet from fear of evil. 33 Don't worry about all these things that are going on; Stay in Jesus and you know you will be safe. So rest in him, however; you will be tempted by Satan and you will be tried. (Romans 7: 19-25) says, 9For the good that I would I do not: but the evil which I would not, that I do. 20Now if I do that I would not, it is no more I that do it, but sin that dwelled in me. 21I find then a law, that, when I would do good, evil is present with me. 22For I delight in the law of God after the inward man: 23But I see another law in my members, warring against the law of my mind, and bringing me into captivity to the law of sin which is in my members. 24O wretched man that I am! Who shall deliver me from the body of this death? 25I thank God through Jesus Christ our Lord. So then with the mind I serve the law of God; but with the flesh the law of sin. 34You don't have to serve sin anymore. (Romans 6: 1-10) says, what shall we say then? Shall we continue in sin, that grace may abound? 2God forbid. How shall we, that are dead to sin, live any longer therein? 3 Know ye not, that so many of us as were baptized into Jesus Christ were baptized into his death? 4Therefore we are buried with him by baptism into death: that like as Christ was raised up from the dead by the glory of the Father, even so we also should walk in newness of life. 5For if we have been planted together in the likeness of his death, we shall be also in the likeness of his resurrection: 6Knowing this, that our old man is crucified with him, that the body of sin might be destroyed, that henceforth we should not serve sin. 7For he that is dead is freed from sin. 8Now if we be dead with Christ, we believe that we shall also live with him: 9Knowing that Christ being raised from the dead diet no more; death hath no more dominion over him. 10For in that he died, he died unto sin once: but in that he lived, he lived unto God. 35So you don't have to walk around condemned because sin will condemn you. (Romans 8: 1-7) says, There is therefore now no condemnation to them which are in Christ Jesus, who walk not after the flesh, but after the Spirit. 2For the law of the Spirit of life in Christ Jesus hath made me free from the law of sin and death. 3For what the law could not do, in that it was weak through the flesh, God sending his own Son in the likeness of sinful flesh, and for sin, condemned sin in the flesh: 4That the righteousness of the law might be fulfilled in us, who walk not after the flesh, but after the Spirit. 5For they that are after the flesh do mind the things of the flesh; but they that are after the Spirit the things of the Spirit. 6For to be carnally minded is death; but to be spiritually minded is life and peace. 7Because the carnal mind is enmity against God: for it is not subject to the law of God, neither indeed can be. 36You can't love two because you don't have time to do what the other one wants you to do. One God will go undone, for somebody. (James 4: 4) says, 4Ye adulterers and adulteresses, know ye not that the friendship of the world is enmity with God? Whosoever therefore will be a friend of the world is the enemy of God.37 Whosoever therefore will be a friend of the world, is the enemy of God.

You can't serve God, not with eye service, as a man pleases, but the servants of Christ. Doing the will of God from the heart, with good will doing service, as to the Lord, and not to men; knowing that whatsoever good things any man does, the same shall he receive of the Lord, whether he be bond or free. (Galatians 3: 28-29) says, there is neither Jew nor Greek, there is neither bond nor free, there is neither male nor female: for ye are all one in Christ Jesus. 29And if ye be Christ's, then are ye Abraham's seed, and heirs according to the promise. 38(Romans 8: 17-) says, 7And if children, then heirs; heirs of God, and joint-heirs with Christ; if so be that we suffer with him, that we may be also glorified together.39 (Philippians 1:29-30) says, For unto you it is given in the behalf of Christ, not only to believe on him, but also to suffer for his sake; 30Having the same conflict which ye saw in me, and now hear to be in me. 40(Hebrews 11: 25) says, 5Choosing rather to suffer affliction with the people of God, than to enjoy the pleasures of sin for a season; 41 Some people can do good things as long as things are going good with them, but when the storms start rising, they give up, but you have to be rooted in the word. (Mark 4: 17-19) says, 7And have no root in themselves, and so endure but for a time: afterward, when affliction or persecution arises for the word's sake, immediately they are offended. 18And these are they which are sown among thorns; such as hear the word, 19And the cares of this world, and the deceitfulness of riches, and the lusts of other things entering in, choke the word, and it becomes unfruitful.42 If you sow among thorns, you shouldn't look for a good crop. It will be choked and dried up. Afterwards, you can't hear the word because your ears are stopped up and your eyes are dim, and you are on the outside looking in. You are not aware of what is going on until God taught you again and filled you over again with the Holy Ghost. Those of you that have ears to hear let them hear what the spirit is saying to the church. (Revelation 10: 1-11) says,1And I saw another mighty angel come down from heaven, clothed with a cloud: and a rainbow was upon his head, and his face was as it were the sun, and his feet as pillars of fire: 2And he had in his hand a little book open: and he set his right foot upon the sea, and his left foot on the earth, 3And cried with a loud voice, as when a lion roared: and when he had cried, seven thunders uttered their voices. 4And when the seven thunders had uttered their voices, I was about to write: and I heard a voice from heaven saying unto me, Seal up those things which the seven thunders uttered, and write them not. 5And the angel which I saw stand upon the sea and upon the earth lifted up his hand to heaven, 6And swore by him that lived for ever and ever, who created heaven, and the things that therein are, and the earth, and the things that therein are, and the sea, and the things which are therein, that there should be time no longer: 7But in the days of the voice of the seventh angel, when he shall begin to sound, the mystery of God should be finished, as he hath declared to his servants the prophets. 8And the voice which I heard from heaven space unto me again, and said, Go and take the little book which is open in the hand of the angel which standout upon the sea and upon the earth. 9And I went unto the angel, and said unto him, Give me the little book. And he said unto me, Take it, and eat it up; and it shall make thy belly bitter, but it shall be in thy mouth sweet as honey. 10And I took the little book out of the angel's hand, and ate it up; and it was in my mouth sweet as honey: and as soon as I had eaten it, my belly was bitter. 11And he said unto me, Thou must prophesy again before many peoples, and nations, and tongues, and kings. 43What is bitter now, it will be sweet after while. We must preach the word, if it hurt, it will help later. You have to hurt to hope. You have to be broken in order to be fixed.

You have to go down in order to have to come back up. When God told the angels to seal up the thunders that were uttered, he didn't say that was all, he said, that he was going to reveal some things to his saints. When God is ready t use you, he takes you through a process to make you, it might hurt you, but it will help you and then you are ready to be used. (Exodus 6:8) says, and I will bring you in unto the land, concerning which I did swear to give it to Abraham, to Isaac, and to Jacob; and I will give it you for an heritage: I am the LORD.44God can do whatever he want to because he is God. We can't finger him out, so don't try. (Exodus 6: 9-14) says, 9And Moses space so unto the children of Israel: but they hearkened not unto Moses for anguish of spirit, and for cruel bondage. 10And the Lord s ace unto Moses, saying, 11Go in, speak unto Pharaoh King of Egypt, which he let the children of

Israel go out of his land. 12And Moses space before the LORD, saying, Behold, the children of Israel have not hearkened unto me; how then shall Pharaoh hear me, who am of uncircumcised lips? 13And the LORD space unto Moses and unto Aaron, and gave them a charge unto the children of Israel, and unto Pharaoh king of Egypt, to bring the children of Israel out of the land of Egypt. 45 This is our commandment today. God is saying, preach unto my people. Bring them up and out of the hands of Satan. We have a charge to keep and a God to glorify. God is saying, go out there in the streets, and deliver my people. It seems like it can't be done, but we need to know, we can't but God can. If God said it, it is already done. (Acts 4: 1-22) says, And as they space unto the people, the priests, and the captain of the temple, and the Sadducees, came upon them, 2Being grieved that they taught the people, and preached through Jesus the resurrection from the dead. 3And they laid hands on them, and put them in hold unto the next day: for it was now eventide. 4Howbeit many of them which heard the word believed; and the number of the men was about five thousand. 5And it came to pass on the morrow, that their rulers, and elders, and scribes, 6And Anna's the high priest, and Caiaphas, and John, and Alexander, and as many as were of the kindred of the high priest, were gathered together at Jerusalem. 7And when they had set them in the midst, they asked, by what power, or by what name, have ye done this? 8Then Peter, filled with the Holy Ghost, said unto them, Ye rulers of the people, and elders of Israel, 9If we this day be examined of the good deed done to the impotent man, by what means he is made whole; 10Be it known unto you all, and to all the people of Israel, that by the name of Jesus Christ of Nazareth, whom ye crucified, whom God raised from the dead, even by him doth this man stand here before you whole. 11This is the stone which was set at naught of you builders, which is become the head of the corner. 12Neither is there salvation in any other: for there is none other name under heaven given among men, whereby we must be saved. 13Now when they saw the boldness of Peter and John, and perceived that they were unlearned and ignorant men, they marveled; and they took knowledge of them, that they had been with Jesus. 14And beholding the man which was healed standing with them, they could say nothing against it. 15But when they had commanded them to go aside out of the council, they conferred among themselves, 16Saying, what shall we do to these men? For that indeed a notable miracle hath been done by them is manifest to all them that dwell in Jerusalem; and we cannot deny it. 17But that it spread no further among the people, let us straightly threaten them that they speak henceforth to no man in this name. 18And they called them, and commanded them not to speak at all nor teach in the name of Jesus. 19But Peter and John answered and said unto them, Whether it be right in the sight of God to hearken unto you more than unto God, judge ye. 20For we cannot but speak the things which we have seen and heard. 21So when they had further threatened them, they let them go, finding nothing how they might punish them, because of the people: for all men glorified God for that which was done. 22For the man was above forty years old, on whom this miracle of healing was showed. 46We can see here that you never get into trouble for doing good things, but we know Jesus will get us out when things begin to come against us. Just know God wants to show his power. When Satan wants you to bow down to him, God wants to make you strong so he can use you. (Daniel 6: 10-28) says, 0Now when Daniel knew that the writing was signed, he went into his house; and his windows being open in his chamber toward Jerusalem, he kneeled upon his knees three times a day, and prayed, and gave thanks before his God, as he did aforetime. 11Then these men assembled, and found Daniel praying and making supplication before his God. 12Then they came near, and space before the king concerning the king's decree; Hast thou not signed a decree, that every man that shall ask a petition of any God or man within thirty days, save of thee, O king, shall be cast into the den of lions? The king answered and said, the thing is true, according to the law of the Medes and Persians, which altered not. 13Then answered they and said before the king, That Daniel, which is of the children of the captivity of Judah, regarded not thee, O king, nor the decree that thou hast signed, but makes his petition three times a day. 14Then the king, when he heard these words, was sore displeased with himself, and set his heart on Daniel to deliver him: and he labored till the going down of the sun to deliver him. 15Then these men assembled unto the king, and said unto the king, Know, O king, that the law of the Medes and Persians is, that no decree nor statute which the king established may be changed. 16Then the king commanded, and they brought Daniel, and cast him into the den of lions. Now the king space and said unto Daniel, Thy God whom thou serves continually, he will deliver thee. 17And a stone was brought, and laid upon the mouth of the den; and the king sealed it with his own signet, and with the signet of his lords; that the purpose might not be changed concerning Daniel. 18Then the king went to his palace, and passed the night fasting: neither were instruments of music brought before him: and his sleep went from him. 19Then the king arose very early in the morning, and went in haste unto the den of lions. 20And when he came to the den, he cried with a lamentable voice unto Daniel: and the king space and said to Daniel, O Daniel, servant of the living God, is thy God, whom thou serves continually, able to deliver thee from the lions? 21Then said Daniel unto the king, O king, live for ever. 22My God hath sent his angel, and hath shut the lions' mouths, that they have not hurt me: forasmuch as before him innocence was found in me; and also before thee, O king, have I done no hurt. 23Then was the king exceeding glad for him, and commanded that they should take Daniel up out of the den.

So Daniel was taken up out of the den, and no manner of hurt was found upon him, because he believed in his God. 24And the king commanded, and they brought those men which had accused Daniel, and they cast them into the den of lions, them, their children, and their wives; and the lions had the mastery of them, and brake all their bones in pieces or ever they came at the bottom of the den. 25Then king Darius wrote unto all people, nations, and languages, that dwell in all the earth; Peace be multiplied unto you. 26I make a decree, that in every dominion of my kingdom men tremble and fear before the God of Daniel: for he is the living God, and steadfast forever, and his kingdom that which shall not be destroyed, and his dominion shall be even unto the end. 27He delivered and rescued, and he worked signs and wonders in heaven and in earth, who hath delivered Daniel from the power of the lions. 28So this Daniel prospered in the reign of Darius, and in the reign of Cyrus the Persian. 47There is only one God, a true and living God. Try yours first, and then try my God, who can answer by fire. That God you made can't answer you in time of trouble. (1King 18: 21-39) says, 1And Elijah came unto all the people, and said, How long halt ye between two opinions? If the LORD be God, follow him: but if Baal, then follow him. And the people answered him not a word. 22Then said Elijah unto the people, I, even I only, remain a prophet of the LORD; but Baal's prophets are four hundred and fifty men. 23Let them therefore give us two bullocks; and let them choose one bullock for themselves, and cut it in pieces, and lay it on wood, and put no fire under: and I will dress the other bullock, and lay it on wood, and put no fire under: 24And call ye on the name of your gods, and I will call on the name of the LORD: and the God that answered by fire, let him be God. And all the people answered and said, it is well spoken. 25And Elijah said unto the prophets of Baal, Choose you one bullock for yourselves, and dress it first; for ye are many; and call on the name of your gods, but put no fire under. 26And they took the bullock which was given them, and they dressed it, and called on the name of Baal from morning even until noon, saying, O Baal, hear us. But there was no voice, nor any that answered. And they leaped upon the altar which was made. 27And it came to pass at noon, that Elijah mocked them, and said, cry aloud: for he is a god; either he is talking, or he is pursuing, or he is in a journey, or peradventure he slept, and must be awaked. 28And they cried aloud, and cut themselves after their manner with knives and lancets, till the blood gushed out upon them. 29And it came to pass, when midday was past, and they prophesied until the time of the offering of the evening sacrifice, that there was neither voice, nor any to answer, nor any that regarded. 30And Elijah said unto all the people, Come near unto me. And all the people came near unto him. And he repaired the altar of the LORD that was broken down. 31And Elijah took twelve stones, according to the number of the tribes of the sons of Jacob, unto whom the word of the LORD came, saying, Israel shall be thy name: 32And with the stones he built an altar in the name of the LORD: and he made a trench about the altar, as great as would contain two measures of seed. 33And he put the wood in order, and cut the bullock in pieces, and laid him on the wood, and said, Fill four barrels with water, and pour it on the burnt sacrifice, and on the wood. 34And he said, Do it the second time. And they did it the second time. And he said, Do it the third time. And they did it the third time. 35And the water ran round about the altar; and he filled the trench also with water. 36And it came to pass at the time of the offering of the evening sacrifice, that Elijah the prophet came near, and said, LORD God of Abraham, Isaac, and of Israel, let it be known this day that thou art God in Israel, and that I am thy servant, and that I have done all these things at thy word. 37Hear me, O LORD, hear me, that this people may know that thou art the LORD God, and that thou hast turned their heart back again. 38Then the fire of the LORD fell, and consumed the burnt sacrifice, and the wood, and the stones, and the dust, and licked up the water that was in the trench. 39And when all the people saw it, they fell on their faces: and they said, The LORD, he is the God; the LORD, he is the God. 48Sometimes we maybe calling on the wrong God or maybe we are calling on him in the wrong time, or maybe we calling on him in the wrong spirit, because he isn't dead, maybe we are dead in the spirit. Let us wake up an then we can hear from God because he said, if we live right, we can ask for what we want. So don't you want the nation healed? Let us ask in him, it is not too late. God wants to show his power. If we can stand on his word when it seems like everything is going wrong, just step back, and let God do it for us. Get out of the way, God don't need any help, he just need us to get back and let him move.

One day somebody is going to say, God is the true and living God. Can't you see things have gotten out of hand with man. It is going to take God to straighten it out. Man have made something to help us, however, it is turning around and killing us. Man is too smart for his own good. So let God do it. It might seem hard, but we must turn back to God if we want him to turn back to us. This goes for the whole nation because God said any nation that turns their back on him, suddenly, he will destroy it. (Jeremiah 27: 7-20) says, 7And all nations shall serve him, and his son, and his son's son, until the very time of his land come: and then many nations and great kings shall serve themselves of him. 8And it shall come to pass, that the nation and kingdom which will not serve the same Nebuchadnezzar the king of Babylon, and that will not put their neck under the yoke of the king of Babylon, that nation will I punish, smith the LORD, with the sword, and with the famine, and with the pestilence, until I have consumed them by his hand. 9Therefore hearken not ye to your prophets, nor to your diviners, nor to your dreamers, nor to your enchanters, nor to your sorcerers, which speak unto you, saying, Ye shall not serve the king of Babylon: 10For they prophesy a lie unto you, to remove you far from your land; and that I should drive you out, and ye should perish. 11But the nations that bring their neck under the yoke of the king of Babylon, and serve him, those will I let remain still in their own land, smith the LORD; and they shall till it, and dwell therein. 12I space also to Zedekiah king of Judah according to all these words, saying, brings your necks under the yoke of the king of Babylon, and serves him and his people, and lives. 13Why will ye die, thou and thy people, by the sword, by the famine, and by the pestilence, as the LORD hath spoken against the nation that will not serve the king of Babylon? 14Therefore hearken not unto the words of the prophets that speak unto you, saying, ye shall not serve the king of Babylon: for they prophesy a lie unto you. 15For I have not sent them, smith the LORD, yet they prophesy a lie in my name; that I might drive you out, and that ye might perish, ye, and the prophets that prophesy unto you. 16Also I space to the priests and to all this people, saying, Thus smith the LORD; Hearken not to the words of your prophets that prophesy unto you, saying, Behold, the vessels of the LORD'S house shall now shortly be brought again from Babylon: for they prophesy a lie unto you. 17Hearken not unto them; serve the king of Babylon, and live: wherefore should this city be laid waste? 18But if they be prophets, and if the word of the LORD be with them, let them now make intercession to the LORD of hosts that the vessels which are left in the house of the LORD, and in the house of the king of Judah, and at Jerusalem, go not to Babylon. 19For thus smith the LORD of hosts concerning the pillars, and concerning the sea, and concerning the bases, and concerning the residue of the vessels that remain in this city, 49 We all have been used by Satan, but let God use what is left of you as long as you are breathing, and in your right mind. God can and he will use you if you let him.(Hebrews 8: 7-13) says, 7For if that first covenant had been faultless, then should no place have been sought for the second. 8For finding fault with them, he smith, Behold, the days come, smith the Lord, when I will make a new covenant with the house of Israel and with the house of Judah: 9Not according to the covenant that I made with their fathers in the day when I took them by the hand to lead them out of the land of Egypt; because they continued not in my covenant, and I regarded them not, smith the Lord. 10For this is the covenant that I will make with the house of Israel after those days, smith the Lord; I will put my laws into their mind, and write them in their hearts: and I will be to them a God, and they shall be to me a people: 11And they shall not teach every man his neighbor, and every man his brother, saying, Know the Lord: for all shall know me, from the least to the greatest. 12For I will be merciful to their unrighteousness, and their sins and their iniquities will I remember no more. 13In that he smith, A new covenant, he hath made the first old. Now that which decayed and waxed old is ready to vanish away. 50God will forgive and forget your sins and iniquities. He said he will not remember anymore, what more do you want? He has laid down the foundation and opened up the way, what more do you want? He came to save that which was lost, then went back to his father, after that he then prayed to his father to send back the Holy Ghost. Can you think of anything else you need and can't get? Live right and name it!!!

God is the biggest man in town, uptown, downtown. (John 10: 9), says, I am the door: by me if any man enter in, he shall be saved, and shall go in and out, and find pasture.51I am the door; if any man comes I he must come by me. I am so high you can't go over me, I am so wide you ant go around me, I am so low you can't go under me. You must come in at the door, because there is no other way you can get there.

God is the baldest man in uptown, downtown, and around town. If you don't believe, go to the books of (Acts 9: 1-5) and it says, 1And Saul, yet breathing out threatening and slaughter against the disciples of the Lord, went unto the high priest, 2And desired of him letters to Damascus to the synagogues, that if he found any of this way, whether they were men or women, he might bring them bound unto Jerusalem. 3And as he journeyed, he came near Damascus: and suddenly there shined round about him a light from heaven: 4And he fell to the earth, and heard a voice saying unto him, Saul, Saul, why persecutes thou me? 5And he said, who art thou, Lord? And the Lord said, I am Jesus whom thou persecute: it is hard for thee to kick against the pricks. 52

God is the baldest man in town, uptown, downtown, and around town. God can speak and man will live. God can speak and man will die. You don't want to kick against God. He has too much power. When God put Saul on the ground, he asked God, What must I do? What will you have me to do and the Lord said, unto him arise and go into the city and it shall be told thee what thou must do. So when you think you are so bad, you better by pass God. He is the baldest man in town.

God is the best man in town. (John 14:6) says, 6Jesus smith unto him, I am the way, the truth, and the life: no man cometh unto the Father, but by me. God said, I love the world, but I can't find no mas to go man bond. Jesus said, Father prepares me a body, and I will go down and redeem man back to you. Jesus came down for thy two generations to redeem man to God; that is love. No greater love. (John 15:13-16) says, Greater love hath no man than this, that a man lay down his life for his friends. 14Ye are my friends, if ye do whatsoever I command you. 15Henceforth I call you not servants; for the servant knows not what his lord doeth: but I have called you friends; for all things that I have heard of my Father I have made known unto you. 16Ye have not chosen me, but I have chosen you, and ordained you, that ye should go and bring forth fruit, and that your fruit should remain: that whatsoever ye shall ask of the Father in my name, he may give it you. 53

God is the smartest man in town. If you don't believe me, go to (Genesis 11: 1-8) it says, and the whole earth was of one language, and of one speech. 2And it came to pass, as they journeyed from the east, that they found a plain in the land of Shinar; and they dwelt there. 3And they said one to another, Go to, let us make brick, and burn them thoroughly. And they had brick for stone, and slime had they for mortar. 4And they said, Go to, let us build us a city and a tower, whose top may reach unto heaven; and let us make us a name, lest we be scattered abroad upon the face of the whole earth. 5And the LORD came down to see the city and the tower, which the children of men built. 6And the LORD said, Behold, the people is one, and they have all one language; and this they begin to do: and now nothing will be restrained from them, which they have imagined to do. 7Go to, let us go down, and there confound their language, that they may not understand one another's speech. 8So the LORD scattered them abroad from thence upon the face of all the earth: and they left off building the city. 54 Sometimes God will not stop you from doing what you want to do, but he will let you do it until you can't do it anymore. If it is not the will of God, it will come down, and no man can stop it from falling. Your plan will not stand, so you don't need to try it again.

ENDNOTES

1 The King James Version, (Cambridge: Cambridge) 1769. 2 The King James Version, (Cambridge: Cambridge) 1769. 3 The King James Version, (Cambridge: Cambridge) 1769. 4 The King James Version, (Cambridge: Cambridge) 1769. 5 The King James Version, (Cambridge: Cambridge) 1769. 6 The King James Version, (Cambridge: Cambridge) 1769. 7 The King James Version, (Cambridge: Cambridge) 1769. 8 The King James Version, (Cambridge: Cambridge) 1769. 9 The King James Version, (Cambridge: Cambridge) 1769. 10 The King James Version, (Cambridge: Cambridge) 1769. 11 The King James Version, (Cambridge: Cambridge) 1769. 12 The King James Version, (Cambridge: Cambridge) 1769. 13 The King James Version, (Cambridge: Cambridge) 1769. 14 The King James Version, (Cambridge: Cambridge) 1769. 15 The King James Version, (Cambridge: Cambridge) 1769. 16 The King James Version, (Cambridge: Cambridge) 1769. 17 The King James Version, (Cambridge: Cambridge) 1769. 18 The King James Version, (Cambridge: Cambridge) 1769. 19 The King James Version, (Cambridge: Cambridge) 1769. 20 The King James Version, (Cambridge: Cambridge) 1769. 21 The King James Version, (Cambridge: Cambridge) 1769. 22 The King James Version, (Cambridge: Cambridge) 1769. 23 The King James Version, (Cambridge: Cambridge) 1769. 24 The King James Version, (Cambridge: Cambridge) 1769. 25 The King James Version, (Cambridge: Cambridge) 1769. 26 The King James Version, (Cambridge: Cambridge) 1769. 27 The King James Version, (Cambridge: Cambridge) 1769. 28 The King James Version, (Cambridge: Cambridge) 1769. 29 The King James Version, (Cambridge: Cambridge) 1769. 30 The King James Version, (Cambridge: Cambridge) 1769. 31 The King James Version, (Cambridge: Cambridge) 1769. 32 The King James Version, (Cambridge: Cambridge) 1769. 33 The King James Version, (Cambridge: Cambridge) 1769. 34 The King James Version, (Cambridge: Cambridge) 1769. 35 The King James Version, (Cambridge: Cambridge) 1769. 36 The King James Version, (Cambridge: Cambridge) 1769. 37 The King James Version, (Cambridge: Cambridge) 1769. 38 The King James Version, (Cambridge: Cambridge) 1769. 39 The King James Version, (Cambridge: Cambridge) 1769. 40 The King James Version, (Cambridge: Cambridge) 1769. 41 The King James Version, (Cambridge:

Cambridge) 1769. 42 The King James Version, (Cambridge: Cambridge) 1769. 43 The King James Version, (Cambridge: Cambridge) 1769. 44 The King James Version, (Cambridge: Cambridge) 1769. 45 The King James Version, (Cambridge: Cambridge) 1769. 46 The King James Version, (Cambridge: Cambridge) 1769. 47 The King James Version, (Cambridge: Cambridge) 1769. 48 The King James Version, (Cambridge: Cambridge) 1769. 49 The King James Version, (Cambridge: Cambridge) 1769. 50 The King James Version, (Cambridge: Cambridge) 1769. 51 The King James Version, (Cambridge: Cambridge) 1769. 52 The King James Version, (Cambridge: Cambridge) 1769. 53 The King James Version, (Cambridge: Cambridge) 1769. 54 The King James Version, (Cambridge: Cambridge) 1769

www.ingramcontent.com/pod-product-compliance
Lightning Source LLC
LaVergne TN
LVHW020438070526
838199LV00063B/4781